How America Benefits From Economic Engagement With India

By

Vinod K. Jain, Ph.D.
Robert H. Smith School of Business
University of Maryland

Kamlesh Jain, Ph.D.
India-US World Affairs Institute, Inc.
Washington, D.C.

Released in Washington D.C. on June 15, 2010
by Congressman James McDermott
at the
East-West Center-FICCI-School of Advanced International Studies Seminar on
U.S.-India Economic Relations: The Road Ahead

Released in Mumbai on July 31, 2010
by the Honorable Kapil Sibal
Union Minister for Human Resource Development
at the
Indo-American Society's
Indo-US Summit on Higher Education

Silver Spring, Maryland

www.india-us.org

Contents

Tables

Figures

Foreword

While popular perception has it that the companies of India Inc. are taking jobs away from Americans and adding little value to the U.S. economy, nothing could be further from the truth. As the authors of this study demonstrate, Indian companies have been investing steadily in the U.S. for decades, and with the rise of India Inc. the magnitude and impact of such investments have increased.

Using India's most successful and venerated company, the Tata Group, as a case study, this report shows how Indian firms are contributing to U.S. economic growth through investment and job creation in America, through mergers and acquisitions of U.S. companies, and through exports of U.S. products and services.

Firms and individuals from India also make a powerful impact on other aspects of U.S. culture and society. Students from India are responsible for a significant portion of the billions of dollars spent annually by foreign students in the United States. Tata and other Indian firms have made significant contributions to U.S. museums and other cultural organizations, to educational institutions, and to other non-profit activities, including post-Katrina relief efforts.

The India-US World Affairs Institute is pleased to have partnered with the Robert H. Smith School of Business, University of Maryland, and with the Federation of Indian Chambers of Commerce & Industry to prepare this report. Its findings, we hope, will foster greater appreciation of the growing importance of India to the U.S., and will remind us how increasingly intertwined are the economies of these two great countries.

Timothy D. Matlack
Chairman
India-US World Affairs Institute, Inc.

Foreword

For too long, the relationship between developed and developing nations had been a one-way street. For decades, vehicles like America's PL 480 program (Public Law 480) provided much needed food aid to developing countries as a means to combat world hunger and malnutrition, and develop export markets for U.S. agricultural commodities and products. In the 1980s and 1990s, development aid by countries was partially replaced by foreign direct and institutional investments by companies. Multinationals from developed countries also began to disseminate technology to junior partners in developing countries, with the idea of using such technology to produce and sell products there.

In the 2000s, we are seeing a dramatic paradigm shift, whereby developing countries are now giving birth to multinationals of their own, and these multinationals are making acquisitions and other investments in developed countries at an accelerating pace. Multinationals from developed countries that went to developing countries to produce and sell products are now leveraging the intellectual capital there to perform research & development and other high value-added work in the developing countries.

This study challenges the received wisdom, the old paradigm, of international economic engagement between developed and developing nations, using the United States and India as a case in point. The study shows how major multinationals from India are now making significant acquisitions and greenfield investments, and creating jobs, in the United States. Some of the Indian companies to which work was being outsourced in the earlier era are now insourcing such jobs within the United States itself, using American workers to perform value-added work.

The challenge in this changed scenario is to find a balance between the interests of developed and developing nations, and between the interests of their respective multinationals.

The Federation of Indian Chambers of Commerce & Industry is pleased to partner with the India-US World Affairs Institute and the Robert H. School of Business, University of Maryland, in this important study. It's my hope that the study will prove to be a lightning rod for greater economic engagement between India and United States and for strengthening our common interests.

Dr. Amit Mitra
Secretary General
Federation of Indian Chambers of Commerce & Industry (FICCI)

Executive Summary

The continual globalization of the American economy evokes widely disparate viewpoints within the United States – from a threat to the American way of life to globalization as a panacea for anything and everything. Clearly, neither view presents an accurate account of reality.

This study investigates one specific aspect of globalization of the American economy, namely, the United States-India business relationship. It provides, for the first time, a comprehensive analysis of America's economic engagement with India for the period 2004 to 2009. The analysis covers India's foreign direct investments into the United States and U.S. exports to India, as well as an assessment of their impacts on the American economy. Also included in the study are the economic impacts Indian Americans are having in the United States.

It presents a case for even stronger business ties between the United States and India. Such a relationship will benefit the United States (and India) especially with regard to jobs, the Number One policy issue in Washington and the Number One livelihood issue on Main Street America today.

The study is more up-to-date and more comprehensive about U.S.-India economic engagement than practically any other study published so far. It is based on a variety of secondary information, including information from world-class sources such as the Financial Times, Thompson SDC Database, and the U.S. Department of Commerce, among others. We also conducted our own research and interviews with several Indian companies in the United States to further explore areas of the study. A summary of the study's key findings is presented below.

India Inc. Goes Abroad

Indian companies have been investing abroad for decades, though the pace of foreign investments has accelerated significantly since 1991, and especially in the 2000s. This development is a result of several factors, including Indian companies' ability to arbitrage their cost advantages, access to a large talent pool, success at home – in a huge domestic market with cut-throat competition, reasonably well-developed institutions (compared to many other emerging markets), business acumen arising from an entrepreneurial tradition, business sophistication, financial market sophistication, production efficiency, a long exposure to Western and Japanese multinationals and their management practices, and Government of India's progressive relaxation of foreign investment rules.

While in the 1960s/1970s/1980s, Indian multinationals were investing in other developing countries, the trend in the last decade has been to go "up market" and they now also invest in highly developed economies like the United States. This portends a reversal of roles whereby developing countries like India are now making investments in developed countries, not just the other way around.

India's Greenfield Investments in the United States

1. During 2004-2009, 90 Indian companies made 127 greenfield investments worth $5.5 billion, and created 16,576 jobs in the United States. The top three destination states for greenfield investments were Minnesota, Virginia, and Texas, in that order. However, the top three states in terms of jobs created were Ohio, Texas, and California.

2. The five U.S. industrial sectors that received the most greenfield investment were Metals; Software & IT Services; Leisure & Entertainment; industrial machinery, equipment & tools; and financial services, accounting for almost 80% of total greenfield investment in the United States. It is noteworthy that the software and IT services sector received less than 15% of total investment, and the bulk of investments went into mining, manufacturing, and other industries.

3. Ten Indian companies made more than 70% of the total $5.5 billion dollars of greenfield investments in the United States:

    - Essar Steel (Minnesota): $1,600 million
    - JSW Steel (N/A): $1,000 million
    - Tata Consultancy Services (California, Michigan, New York, Ohio): $273.4 million
    - Welspun Group (Arkansas; Texas): $246 million
    - Reliance Adlabs (Illinois): $161 million
    - Indage Group (Virginia): $160.5 million
    - HCL Group (New Jersey): $148.7 million
    - Flag Telecom, Reliance (N/A): $124.1 million
    - Tata Communications (Virginia): $102.7 million
    - PSL (Mississippi): $100 million

India's Mergers and Acquisitions in the United States

1. During 2004-2009, 239 Indian companies made 372 acquisitions in the United States. We were able to obtain the deal value for only 267 of these transactions. The total value of the 267 acquisitions was $21 billion, or $78.7 million per acquisition.

2. Of these 267 acquisitions, we were able to obtain the numbers of jobs created/saved for only 85 transactions, which came to over 40,000 jobs. (The total number of jobs created or saved by all 372 transactions must be much higher).

3. Five states that attracted the most M&A investments from Indian companies accounted for 75% of total deal value: Georgia, New Jersey, Michigan, California, and Texas.

4. The five leading U.S. sectors receiving M&A investments from India were: Manufacturing; IT & IT Enabled Services; Biotech, Chemicals & Pharmaceuticals; Automotive; and Telecom – for a total of 83% of total deal value. The bulk of M&A investments by India Inc. in the United States were in manufacturing and other industrial sectors, rather than in services for which India is well known.

The value of U.S. acquisitions by Indian companies fell in 2008 and then again in 2009 even more steeply, a result of the worldwide recession. It is however interesting to note that greenfield investments rose through 2008, achieving their highest level that year, and then registered a decline in 2009, though the decline was not as steep as for acquisitions. This is possibly because making a greenfield investment is a longer-term decision, while acquisitions are often opportunistic and accomplished relatively more quickly.

U.S. Exports to India

1. The United States-India goods trade tripled during 2004-2008. American merchandise exports to India during the same period grew at a compounded annual growth rate of over 30 percent. As a result of the global recession, U.S. exports to India declined slightly in 2009.

2. For the period 2004-2009, U.S. exports to India grew by a total of 269 percent, while India's exports to the United States grew by 136 percent. U.S. exports to India have grown faster than exports to practically all other countries in the world.

3. U.S. manufactured exports to India were linked to 96,000 manufacturing and non-manufacturing jobs in the U.S. in 2009. Ten states (California, Washington, Texas, Illinois, New York, Utah, Pennsylvania, South Carolina, Florida, and Georgia) accounted for only 62 percent of all U.S. jobs linked to exports to India in 2009, indicating that the benefits of exporting to India are wide spread throughout the nation.

These numbers do not include agricultural, mining, and services exports, which will have their own implications for jobs in the United States. For instance, in 2007 the United States exported services worth $9.4 billion to India, compared to the goods worth $15 billion that are the focus of our study.

Immigrant Entrepreneurs, Professionals and Students from India

The 2.57 million Indian Americans in the United States contribute to the U.S. economy and society in numerous ways. It's hard to measure their economic impact with any precision. Here are some pointers in that direction.

1. A 2007 joint Duke University-UC Berkeley study found that Indian immigrant entrepreneurs had founded more engineering and technology companies during 1995-2005 than immigrants from Britain, China, Japan, and Taiwan combined.

2. A 2007 study by the National Venture Capital Association (NVCA) found that India was the most common place of birth for foreign-born founders of venture capital-backed public companies, followed by Britain, China, Iran, and France.

3. The list of major companies whose founders or co-founders are of Indian heritage include Akamai (1,750 employees), Bose Corporation (8,000 employees), iGate (6,910 employees), Kanbay International (6,900 employees), Sun Microsystems (29,000 employees), and Syntel (13,600 employees). Dozens of such companies in the United States have created tens of thousands of jobs.

4. There are currently almost 10,000 Indian American owners of hotels/motels in the United States, who together own over 21,000 hotels with 1.8 million guest rooms and property valued at $129 billion. They employ 578,600 workers.

5. There are about 50,000 physicians (and 15,000 medical students) of Indian heritage in the United States, serving in cities, rural, and peripheral areas throughout the country. They continue to make major contributions to their communities, to healthcare, and to the medical profession in the United States.

6. Education is one of America's finest exports. The foreign students who come for higher studies to the United States not only bring talent, but also contribute to the U.S. economy via tuition and living and other expenses. The expenses incurred by foreign students in the United States are treated as "deemed exports," with implications for thousands of jobs linked to such exports.

   India has had the largest number of foreign students in the U.S. among all countries of origin for eight years in a row. In 2008, there were 94,563 students from India whose net contribution to the U.S. economy was $2.39 billion.

All in all, the study shows how America benefits from economic engagement with India and with people of Indian origin. It has highlighted only the economic and employment benefits of such engagement to the United States, which of course are the biggest issues facing the United States today. However, the non-economic benefits of engaging with India are equally significant – cultural, social, regional security, and political advantages to name just a few.

The State Department, Open Investment, and American Jobs

Obama Administration's Official Position on Inward FDI and U.S. Exports

Fact Sheet

BUREAU OF ECONOMIC, ENERGY AND BUSINESS AFFAIRS
Washington, DC
October 6, 2009

Foreign direct investment (FDI) is an important source of economic growth and job creation in the United States and around the globe. It is vital to U.S. prosperity.

In the past decade, the stock of U.S. direct investment abroad has more than tripled (increasing from $1 trillion in 1998 to $3.2 trillion in 2008). The stock of FDI in the United States totaled $2.3 trillion (about 15.8% of U.S. GDP in 2008).

- In 2006, FDI directly or indirectly contributed to 9.3% of U.S. GDP ($1.25 trillion).
    - Inbound FDI totaled $237.1 billion (1.8% of GDP). Mergers and acquisitions of existing U.S. firms accounted for the vast majority (90%) of new FDI outlays in 2006.
    - U.S. companies earned $322.6 billion from overseas direct investments and remitted $101.7 billion (0.8%) of GDP) to U.S. parent firms in the form of dividends.
    - 19.5% of U.S. exports ($200 billion, 1.5% of GDP) were shipped to foreign subsidiaries of U.S. firms.
    - Nearly 20% of U.S. exports ($204billion, 1.6% of GDP) were shipped from U.S. affiliates of foreign firms.
    - U.S. affiliates of foreign firms spent $395.8 billion (3.1% of GDP) compensating U.S. employees and $37.8 billion (0.3% of GDP) on research and development. Foreign affiliates also reinvested $69 billion (0.5% of GDP of their earnings in the U.S. economy.
- U.S. exports support millions of American jobs. About 19.9% of all jobs in America's manufacturing sector depend on exports.
- In 2006, U.S. affiliates of foreign companies employed 5.3 million Americans.

The United States has a significant stake, as both the world's largest source and recipient of foreign direct investment, in working with our economic partners both multilaterally and bilaterally to implement policies that facilitate global investment flows. The State Department encourages nondiscriminatory, open, and market-oriented environments for U.S. investment abroad through a wide range of bilateral and multilateral initiatives, including the Organization for Economic Cooperation and Development (OECD) Freedom of Investment project, the G-8 Heiligendamm process, the UN Conference on Trade and Development (UNCTAD), and the Asia-Pacific Economic Cooperation forum (APEC). State and the Office of the United States Trade Representative share negotiation of bilateral investment treaties (BITs) that establish rules that protect the rights of American investors abroad and provide market access for future American investment. The State Department also works closely with the Commerce Department's Invest in America program, which promotes foreign direct investment to the United States.

An open investment climate helps ensure that American citizens continue to reap the benefits associated with inward investment. Through its role as a member of the Committee on Foreign Investment in the United States (CFIUS), the inter-agency panel which reviews the national security implications of certain cross-border mergers and acquisitions (M&As), the State Department and other CFIUS agencies seek to ensure protection of U.S. national security interests while maintaining an open environment for international investment. In 2008, CFIUS concluded action on more than 150 transactions, reflecting over $200 billion in inward U.S. investment.

Source: U.S. Department of State and U.S. Department of Commerce
http://www.state.gov/e/eeb/rls/fs/2009/130371.htm

Section 1. Introduction

> *"Foreign companies are a boon to the American marketplace for the jobs they create, the capital they infuse, the skills they teach, and the opportunities they afford managers, workers, and the executives alike. But that's not all. By spurring competition, fostering innovation, introducing new technologies, and creating newer, better, and even cheaper products, foreign companies are also exerting a powerful and positive impact not only on the careers of employees and managers, but also on the American marketplace as a whole."*
>
> - Micheline Maynard, *The Selling of the American Economy: How Foreign Companies are Remaking the American Dream*, Broadway Books, 2009

Tata, the quintessential Indian conglomerate, came to the United States in 1939 and set up a permanent office in New York City in 1945. Now, more than 70 years later, thirteen Tata companies have a presence in the United States, and over 15,500 Tata employees in almost 100 locations in 43 states are contributing to the U.S. economy and society.

Tata has brought to the United States billions of dollars in capital, created or saved thousands of jobs directly, and many thousands more indirectly. It has ushered in new business models and management expertise, invested in research and development, lowered the cost of products for American consumers and of inputs for American companies, and much else. In addition, some Tata companies in the U.S. export to other countries which links directly to American jobs. And, as the case study later in this section shows, Tata systematically contributes to the communities where it does business.

Though Indian companies, both small and large, have been coming and contributing to the United States economy for decades, the pace of India Inc.'s American entry and contributions has significantly increased in the last few years. This is the subject matter for this report. We present information on hundreds of Indian companies that are now in the United States and how they are contributing to the U.S. economy. A second aspect of this report relates to exports from different U.S. states to India, which correlates positively with jobs in those states. Finally, the study highlights contributions by immigrants and non-immigrants (e.g., students) of Indian ethnicity to the United States economy and society.

This definitive study of the United States' economic engagement with India presents a comprehensive analysis of investments from India into the United States and exports from the U.S. to India – for six years, 2004-2009. It is based on a variety of published information, information available from world-class sources such as the Financial Times, Thompson SDC Database, and the U.S. Department of Commerce, among others, as well as our own research including interviews with a few Indian companies investing in the United States.

Foreign Companies in America

Foreign companies have always played a pivotal role in business and life in America. According to the latest available survey from the U.S. Department of Commerce, U.S. affiliates of foreign-owned companies employed more than five million American workers in 2006. "That is 4.6 percent of the private workforce, up from 3.4 percent twenty years ago… Two million workers are employed by manufacturing affiliates – more than one in eight U.S. factory workers... In 2006, 325,000 Americans worked for foreign affiliates in the motor vehicles and parts sector alone, 278,000 in chemicals, and 180,000 in nonmetallic mineral products such as cement."[i]

Foreign companies often locate their operations and employment in non-metro areas – areas that tend to have higher unemployment levels (and lower cost of doing business). And, Indian companies, more often than not, are investing to create and sustain manufacturing capabilities in the United States, rather than in services for which they are well known.

Essar Steel Limited of India, for instance, acquired Minnesota Steel LLC in 2007 and is investing $1.6 billion to construct a new vertically integrated steel mill in Minnesota's Iron Range. It will be the first facility in North America to include iron ore mining, ore processing, direct reduction, and steelmaking capabilities at a single site.[ii]

At the groundbreaking ceremony on September 19, 2008, Madhu Vuppuluri, President of Essar North America, said, "Together with Minnesota Steel and Algoma Steel, we are optimistic abou creating a new and vibrant steel manufacturing capability in North America."

Figure 1-1: Governor Tim Pawlenty at the groundbreaking ceremony of Essar Steel on September 19, 2008

(MPR Photo/Bob Kelleher)

> Excerpt from Minnesota Governor Tim Pawlenty's speech at the groundbreaking ceremony:
>
> *"What we're doing today, in the midst of a lot of economic turmoil, is celebrating a very substantial success for this region, and for our state, and really for the whole country."*

American affiliates of foreign-owned enterprises tend to be more innovative than domestic companies, and in 2006, they spent $34 billion on R&D, accounting for 14 percent of all R&D performed by U.S. businesses. They also accounted for 19 percent of all U.S. exports. Both these percentages are significantly higher than the percentage of American workers (4.6 percent) who work for foreign companies in the United States. It's no wonder that foreign companies' U.S. affiliates pay much higher salaries (average of $63,400 per year) to their workers than the U.S. average of $48,200 per year.[iii]

Three-fourths of the foreign-affiliate R&D is concentrated in manufacturing, particularly in chemicals, motor vehicles, and pharmaceuticals. This is especially notable since many American companies are relocating their manufacturing – and R&D – to other countries.

When foreign-owned companies make investments in the United States, the media typically focuses the investment dollars they bring in and the numbers of jobs they create or retain (save). However, the role they play in the American economy far exceeds the initial investment or the jobs created. Investing in a foreign market is generally not a one-time occurrence; it often leads to repeat investments in the host market over the next few years and contributes to state and federal taxation revenues. Jain Irrigation Systems of India, for example, acquired Aquarius Brands of Fresno, CA, in February 2007 for $1.80 million. Subsequently, they invested an additional $13.35 million in Fresno and Winterhaven, FL, and paid $574,000 in payroll taxes for 2008. Furthermore, Aquarius Brands (now Jain Irrigation) invested $3.88 million in R&D and had exports of $15 million in 2008.[iv]

U.S. Exports

It's a truism that exports from a country are a result of real jobs in the country, and export growth leads to job and economic growth in the exporting country. When President Barack Obama left for his four-nation tour of Asia on November 12, 2009, his administration officials stressed the importance of Asia to U.S. economic growth. "Right now, 1.6 million jobs in the United States are associated with exports to Asia," said Jeffrey Bader, National Security Council senior director for East Asian Affairs. Asia is "the fastest-growing region in the world," with 7 percent growth expected in the next year. "It already takes about a quarter of our exports, and those exports are expected to increase as the region grows… And, so, we see a lot of jobs being created through our engagement in Asia."[v]

President Obama's stated goal is to double U.S. exports over the next five years and create two million new jobs in the United States. This will likely be achieved through exports to emerging markets more than to America's traditional big trade partners. Among emerging markets, India offers the best prospects for significantly increasing U.S. exports and creating jobs.

United States merchandise exports to India have grown rapidly in the last six years, and tripled from 2004 to 2008. Over this period of time, United States exports to India had the highest growth (200 percent) compared to U.S. exports to practically any other country, including developed countries and other large developing countries (e.g., Brazil, China, and Russia). Tens of thousands of American jobs are linked to exports to India and the count is rising with the trend of increasing exports to India.

The Impact of Immigrant Entrepreneurs, Professionals, and International Students

Immigrants have always contributed handsomely to the U.S. economy through job and wealth creation. The same is true of immigrant entrepreneurs, professionals, and students from India.

This report highlights the contributions made by such individuals in the United States. It includes Indian immigrants like Vinod Khosla who, as co-founder of Sun Microsystems, created tens of thousands of high-technology, high-paying jobs in the United States, and continues to do so in his current role as a venture capitalist. And, it includes the contributions of over 10,000 Indian American hotel owners.

Also included in this report are other professionals, like doctors, engineers, scientists, technologists, and educators, who are contributing to the U.S. economy in numerous ways. In particular, we highlight the roles played by Indian Institutes of Technology (IIT) graduates and members of the American Association of Physicians from India.

Another rarely considered export is the export of education services from the United States. Education is one of America's finest exports and is a trillion dollar industry. The foreign students who come to the U.S. for higher studies not only bring talent, but also contribute to the U.S. economy via tuition, living, and other expenses. According to the Institute of International Education's publication, *Open Doors 2009*, the *net* contribution of foreign students and their families to the U.S. economy in 2008 was over $15.5 billion. Money spent by foreign students and their families in the United States is treated as "deemed exports" from the U.S., which, again, is linked to tens of thousands of American jobs. India has traditionally had the largest numbers of foreign students studying in the United States.[vi]

About the Report

This report is the outcome of a project undertaken by the India-US World Affairs Institute, in association with the Robert H. Smith School of Business, University of Maryland, and the Federation of Indian Chambers of Commerce & Industry (FICCI). Unlike many previous publications on this theme, which focused only on Indian companies' acquisitions in the U.S., this study presents the first comprehensive look at how America benefits from economic engagement with India in multiple spheres. In addition to mergers and acquisitions by Indian companies, the report includes their greenfield investments in the U.S., exports from the U.S. to India, and the impact of Indian American entrepreneurs and other Indian professionals on the U.S. economy.

Project scope did not include the impact of many other ways in which Indian companies are contributing to the United States, such as licensing of U.S. technologies and brands, and acquisitions by Indian companies of U.S. companies' exclusively-foreign operations. Hence, this study does not include the impact of such Indian companies' investments in the U.S. on job creation/retention, for example,

- Purchase of India rights for the Dobutrex brand by Nicholas Piramal India Limited from Eli Lilly & Co. in 2004.

- Purchase of a 50% stake in Omimex de Colombia (with operations in Colombia) by ONGC of India for $425M from the Texas-based Omimex Resources Inc. in 2006.

The remainder of the report is organized into the following key sections:

Section 2. Greenfield investments by Indian companies in the U.S.

Section 3. Mergers and acquisitions by Indian companies in the U.S.

Section 4. U.S. exports to India

Section 5. Impact of immigrant entrepreneurs, professionals, and students from India in America.

Many sections also include one or more case studies that focus on specific companies and their contributions in the United States. These sections are followed by appendices containing a Methodology section, acknowledgements, and information on report authors, the India-US World Affairs Institute, FICCI, and Robert H. Smith School of Business, University of Maryland.

Case Study: Tata in America

The Tata Group, established in 1868, is India's largest and most respected business group with current revenues in excess of $70 billion. The Group has about 90 companies and employs 350,000 people in 80 countries, and its products and services are available in over 120 countries. Tata's businesses include luxury hotels, consumer goods, mining, steel manufacturing, telecommunications, trucks and cars, electric power, credit cards, chemicals, engineering, and IT services and business process outsourcing. Tata is the largest India-headquartered multinational business group in the United States, operating 13 companies with over 15,500 staff in 43 states and the District of Columbia. Tata is contributing to the American economy and society in numerous ways including by reversing the outsourcing trend – bringing jobs back to the United States via insourcing.

Tata's core values of integrity, understanding, excellence, unity, and responsibility are institutionalized within the Group and are fundamental enablers of Tata's global success. Tata is well-known for its unique model of returning wealth to the communities in which it operates. In fact, 66 percent of the holding company Tata Sons' equity capital is owned by philanthropic trusts. In an article about the founder, Jamsetji Tata, Harvard Business School historian N.S.B. Gras wrote, "he saw clearly that the business man was in effect but a trustee of wealth (of the people)."[vii] According to R. Gopalakrishnan, an executive director of Tata Sons Ltd. and a director of several Tata companies, "In a free enterprise, the community is not just another stakeholder in business, but is in fact, the very purpose of its existence." [viii]

Tata first came to the U.S. in 1939 and established a New York branch of the Tata Iron and Steel Company in 1945. The Tata Group now operates a variety of businesses in nearly 100 locations across the United States. Tata grew via both acquisitions and organically, and now owns global brands such as Tetley Tea, Eight O'Clock coffee, Jaguar Land Rover automobiles, Corus Steel, Ritz Carlton (now Taj) Boston, and the Pierre Hotel in New York.[ix]

Table 1-1: Number of Tata Employees by State

The 26 States with More Than 100 Tata Employees Each

State	No. of Employees	State	No. of Employees
New Jersey	1,686	Georgia	384
California	1,647	Indiana	384
New York	1,549	Washington	365
Ohio	1,173	Arizona	329
Texas	1,008	Minnesota	321
Illinois	956	Virginia	267
North Carolina	867	Maryland	216
Florida	599	Colorado	193
Michigan	598	Rhode Island	183
Wyoming	485	Kentucky	168
Connecticut	470	District of Columbia	166
Massachusetts	453	Wisconsin	150
Pennsylvania	409	Delaware	111

Source: Tata Sons Limited, November 2009

In the United States, Tata operates in six business sectors, namely, information systems and communications, engineering, materials, services, consumer products, and chemicals. Table 1.1 shows the 26 U.S. states with the largest numbers of Tata employees currently.

Over the last five years, the Tata Group has invested more than $3 billion in the United States. Annually, Tata reinvests over half a billion dollars in the U.S. economy through research & development programs, capital expenditures, employee salaries, travel, taxes, etc.

Continuing its long tradition of giving back to local communities, Tata supports local and national causes as well as university collaborations. Recent examples include:

- In 2009, Tata Business Support Services (TBSS) and Tata Sons donated 1,500 new books to the 750 students of East Milton Elementary School in Florida under the auspices of Tata's national CSR (corporate social responsibility) partnership with First Book®.
- In 2008, Tata created a $50 million endowment at Cornell University to advance the research and study of agriculture and nutrition in India.

- In 2008, Tata Sons established a student internship program with the University of California, Berkeley that sends students to India to work within local communities on Tata-sponsored community development projects.

- In 2008, three Tata companies jointly committed to a three-year gift to the Foundation of Appalachian Ohio. In addition to providing access to education throughout the 32 Appalachian Ohio counties, the Tata gift will enable eight elementary schools to welcome a traveling science program into their schools.

- In 2007 and 2008, thirty Harvard University undergraduate and graduate students were presented with Tata study grants to pursue academic projects in India and neighboring countries.

- Tata employees support both the Toys for Tots and Adopt-a-Soldier programs in the Washington D.C. area.

- Tata companies sponsored the opening of a Mughal Art exhibition at the Smithsonian Institution in Washington DC and funded website digitization of the Indian miniature paintings collection at the Boston Museum of the Fine Arts.

Tata's U.S. strategy is a combination of greenfield investments and mergers and acquisitions (M&As) with successful U.S. brands where both companies benefit by sharing best practices and blending their respective strengths. In some cases, the acquired companies were ailing and the acquisition enabled recovery that led to not only the retention but also the creation of new American jobs. The following examples illustrate the diverse ways in which Tata companies are contributing to the U.S. economy.

Tata Consultancy Services (TCS) is a 143,000-employee IT services, business solutions, and outsourcing company that operates in 42 countries. In 1979 TCS was the first Indian technology firm to set up operations in New York City.

Today, TCS America provides consulting services to 49 of the Fortune 100 companies. It has 23 offices in the U.S. and employs more than 12,000 staff in 43 states, constituting 80% of the Tata workforce in the United States. Since 2004, TCS America has made greenfield investments of about $135 million in Ohio, Michigan, California, and New York establishing world-class facilities to house IT consultants who provide enterprise systems implementation, networking, and other information technology consulting services, as well as business process outsourcing (BPO) and traditional management consulting services.

Like most Tata companies, TCS takes community service seriously. Notably TCS America now donates 50 cents of every dollar of American profits to charities like the March of Dimes, the American Cancer Society, and to community organizations in the cities where it operates.

In March 2008, TCS opened its first North American domestic delivery center, TCS Seven Hills Park, in Cincinnati, Ohio, with space for 1,000 consultants. On November 5, 2009, at an event attended by Ohio's Governor, Ted Strickland, TCS announced that it had already scaled up to 300 associates. Governor Strickland commented, "Fostering job creation is vital to a strong economic recovery for Ohio. Companies like Tata Consultancy Services are tapping into our highly talented workforce and world-class educational institutions to grow their business while providing high skilled jobs for Ohioans. This is the type of investment and long term commitment that will ensure Ohio's place as an economic leader."

> *"Indeed, to a degree, the process through which the U.S. exported jobs is now being inverted. In November, Ted Strickland, the governor of Ohio, one of the states hit hardest by globalization, showed up at a corporate campus in Milford, a suburb of Cincinnati, to celebrate the fact that Tata Consultancy Services, the Indian outsourcing giant, now employs 300 workers at its North America Domestic Delivery Center. The outsourcer has become an insourcer. Perhaps we're not seeing deglobalization, but rather reglobalization."*
>
> The Vogue for Local by Daniel Gross, *Newsweek International*, 21 December 2009

One example of its humanitarian work is that TCS matched its employees' individual contributions of $50,000 toward relief efforts after Hurricane Katrina. TCS also provided significant and timely pro bono assistance in Louisiana, Mississippi, and Texas. Within days of the hurricane, TCS, working jointly with the Mississippi Department of Employment Security, designed, developed and deployed Mississippi's self service Disaster Unemployment Assistance System for the residents of Mississippi. The system enabled residents to file for unemployment and other emergency funds in that time of crisis.

California-based **Good Earth Teas** offers a wide range of herbal, fruit-flavored, medicinal and specialty green and black teas sold across the nation in grocery, gourmet, and natural food stores. Tata purchased Good Earth in 2005 for $31 million to complement its acquisition of the British tea giant, Tetley in 2000. After the acquisition, Good Earth Teas started managing all Tata U.S. tea business under Tetley Tea. The collaboration has worked well – Good Earth had expertise in producing in-demand products in the U.S. and Tata brought expertise in building efficiencies and expanding distribution globally. The tea continues to be blended and packed in Santa Cruz, California. Since joining the Tata Group, Good Earth Teas has expanded its distribution into new segments with its new Organic range, new retail channels, and new markets like the U.K. and Canada. The increased volume of tea production and management has led to growth in the company's employee base to 70 employees in California, New Jersey, and Georgia.

Good Earth is a green company which packages its tea in 100% recycled materials. The company also works closely with American Forests, one of America's oldest conservation organizations. Through their ongoing partnership and grant program, Good Earth has helped American Forests plant over 20,000 trees. Planting these trees will remove 6,667 tons of CO_2

from the atmosphere over a 50-year span, the equivalent of removing 900 automobiles from U.S. highways.

The Boston Ritz Carlton overlooking Boston Commons has hosted generations of blue blood weddings, debutante balls, christening ceremonies, and mother-daughter afternoon teas. Tata's hotel group acquired the Boston Ritz for $170 million in 2007 and has since renamed it the Taj. Despite initial local concerns about the acquisition of a historic American property by an Indian company, the Taj is flourishing. The company made special efforts to retain staff and preserve the original character of the landmark while improving it by adding luxurious amenities like butlers who could run baths or stoke the existing wood-burning fireplaces in guest rooms. The Taj employs 286 staff in Massachusetts and donates to the Emerald Necklace Conservancy, a nonprofit group that helps maintain the Boston Commons.

In addition to the Taj, Tata's hotel group has invested $67 million to acquire two other well-known hotels with cultural significance to their respective cities – the Campton Place Hotel in San Francisco and the Pierre Hotel in New York.

Section 2. Greenfield Investments by Indian Companies in the United States

"It's all so simple, Anjin-san. Just change your concept of the world."

- James Clavell, *Shōgun*, Dell, 1975

While Indian companies have been investing abroad since the 1970s, the pace of their foreign direct investments increased after the 1991 economic reforms when the Indian economy began opening up to global competition. In the earlier era, Indian companies typically invested in other developing countries, often using vehicles like minority joint ventures, a requirement of the Government of India at the time. However, since the 1990s, and especially in the 2000s, some two-thirds of India Inc.'s foreign direct investments (FDI) have gone "up-market" – to highly developed countries, such as the United States and the United Kingdom. Indian companies have gone abroad using majority joint ventures and wholly-owned subsidiaries, via acquisitions and greenfield investments.[x]

India Inc.'s investments in developed countries result from several factors, including Indian companies' ability to arbitrage their cost advantages; India's human capital, both technical and managerial; a huge domestic market with cut-throat competition in many industries; well-developed institutions (compared to many other emerging markets), such as capital markets and the rule of law; business acumen resulting from entrepreneurial traditions; business sophistication; financial market sophistication;[xi] production efficiency; and a long exposure Western and Japanese multinationals and management practices. Government of India's progressive relaxation of foreign exchange controls, which now allows Indian companies to invest up to 300 percent of their adjusted net worth without prior approval, also enabled them to enter into larger deals.

Indian companies' investments in the United States were also facilitated by the low valuations, bankruptcy auctions, and distress sales of American companies in the last 2-3 years that created many acquisition opportunities in the U.S. According to IMaCS VIRTUS Global Partners, more than half of Indian companies' acquisitions in the United States were because of such reasons.[xii]

All of this is, to a large extent, a reversal of roles. Traditionally, it was the multinationals from developed countries that made FDI into developing countries, though the bulk of FDI from developed countries went into other developed countries. Now, in the 2000s, we are seeing an increasing amount of FDI from developing countries to developed countries. The UNCTAD's *World Investment Report* for 2006 focused on the rise of FDI by transnational corporations (TNCs) from developing and transition economies. According to the report, "New sources of FDI are emerging among developing and transition economies. This phenomenon has been particularly marked in the past ten years, and a growing number of TNCs from these economies are emerging as major regional – or sometimes even global – players. The new links these TNCs are forging with the rest of the world will have far-reaching repercussions in shaping the global economic landscape of the coming decades."[xiii]

This section focuses on Indian companies' *greenfield investments* in the United States, a topic unexplored by similar studies in the past. (Indian companies' mergers and acquisitions in the United States are discussed in the next section). While foreign acquisitions of American companies save or create American jobs, greenfield investments exclusively *create* jobs in America. A greenfield investment involves, by definition, establishing a new operation, which leads to new job creation.

The data included in this report provide a comprehensive picture of Indian companies' greenfield investments in the United States, over a six-year period, 2004-2009. The bulk of this analysis is based on greenfield investment and related job-creation data obtained from fDi Intelligence,[xiv] a subsidiary of the *Financial Times* of U.K., which captures such data for most countries. It is the exclusive source of FDI project data for the UNCTAD *World Investment Report* and the Economist Intelligence Unit.[xv] (See also the Methodology appendix for more details).

Main Findings

This section discusses greenfield investments over the last six years and provides insights into these investments by location, sector, and company as well as trends for investments, jobs, and projects over time.

Figure 2-1: The Top Ten U.S. Sectors Receiving Greenfield Investments from India, 2004-2009

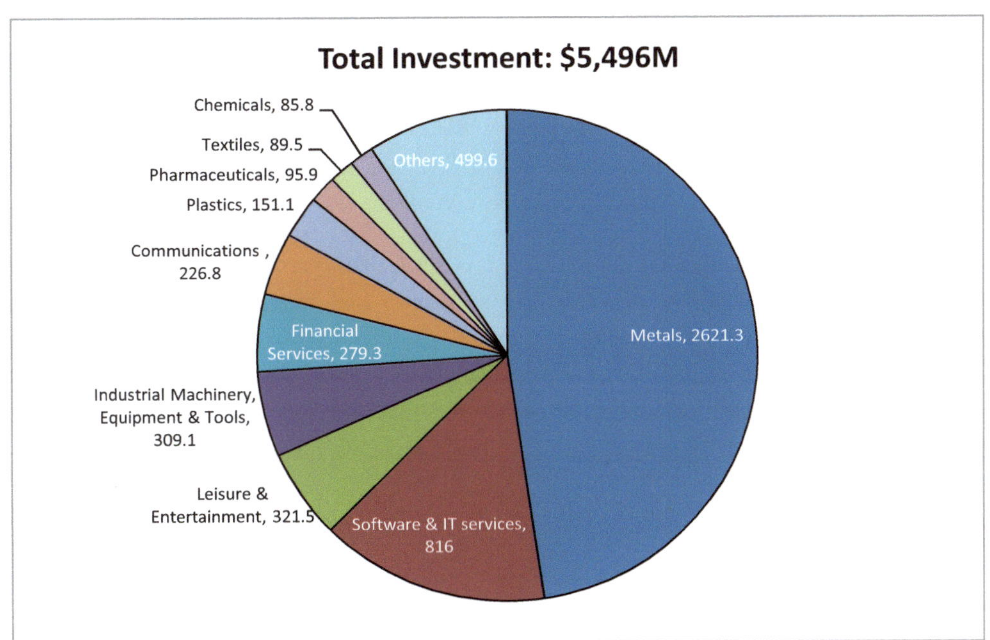

Source: fDi Intelligence, Financial Times Ltd., U.K.

Between January 2004 and December 2009, 90 Indian companies invested almost $5.5 billion through 127 greenfield projects in the United States. Figure 2-1 highlights the major industry sectors in which Indian companies have invested.

Five sectors, Metals, Software & IT Services, Leisure & Entertainment, Industrial Machinery, Equipment & Tools, and Financial Services, comprise about 80 percent of all greenfield investment in the United States. A significant portion of the investment in the metals sector came from a greenfield investment of $1.6 billion for an integrated steel project on IronRange in Minnesota. (See also the Essar Steel case study later in this section).

Figure 2-2, shows the number of greenfield projects undertaken by Indian companies in the United States over the last six years. The six-year annual trend of projects is fairly constant – an average of 21 projects initiated each year.

Figure 2-2: Project Trend Analysis

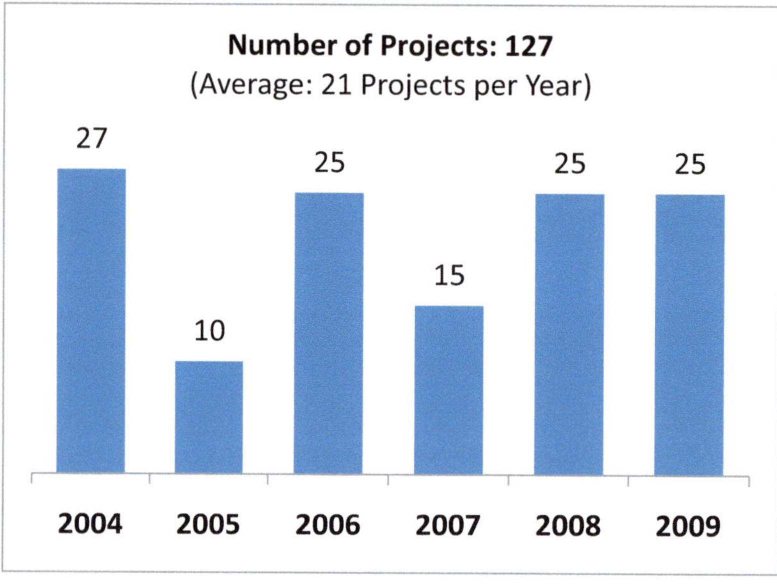

Source: fDi Intelligence, Financial Times Ltd.

The next table, Table 2-1, displays the Top 15 States that received the largest greenfield investments from India. The table also shows the number of jobs created by these investments. Minnesota, Virginia, and Texas account for more than 40 percent of all greenfield investments in the United States. In terms of job creation, five states (Ohio, Texas, California, Illinois, and New Jersey), account for about 45 percent of all jobs created by Indian companies' greenfield investments.

Table 2-1: The Top Fifteen U.S. States Receiving Greenfield Investments from India, 2004-2009

State Rank	Recipient State	Total Amount of FDI ($M)	Number of Investments	Number of Jobs Created
1	Minnesota	1,600.0	1	700
2	Virginia	326.2	6	633
3	Texas	307.5	14	1,799
4	New Jersey	302.6	11	806
5	Ohio	283.8	4	2,329
6	Illinois	243.8	6	1,035
7	California	234.6	19	1,435
8	Arkansas	180.0	2	550
9	New York	174.9	13	523
10	Maryland	101.0	2	308
11	Mississippi	100.0	1	275
12	Georgia	64.8	6	702
13	Florida	32.3	4	150
14	Kentucky	32.0	1	106
15	Louisiana	29.9	2	141
Total (Incl. State Not Specified)		**5,495.9**	**127**	**16,576**

Source: fDi Intelligence, Financial Times Ltd., U.K.

Figure 2-3 shows that Indian companies invested almost $5.5 billion in 127 greenfield projects over the last six years. On average, this equates to $916 million per year, or $43.3 million per greenfield project. Despite the onset of worldwide recession in 2007, the annual total value of greenfield investments continued to rise through 2008, though investments have declined significantly in 2009. During the same period, the average value of greenfield investments per project has dropped significantly from $113.3 million per project in 2007, to $78.1 million per project in 2008, and to $33.0 million per project in 2009 – reflecting the impact of recession on Indian companies' investments.

Figure 2-3: Investment Analysis

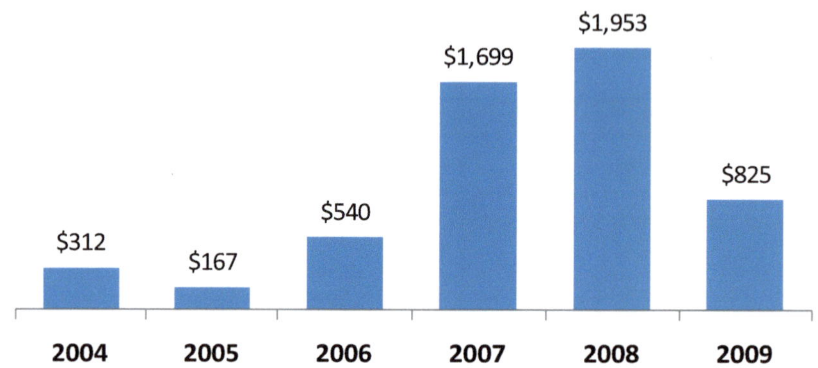

Source: Investment data based on both actual and estimated values, provided by fDi Intelligence, Financial Times Ltd., U.K.

Figure 2-4 shows that 16,576 jobs were created by Greenfield investments over the last six years. That equates to 2,763 jobs per year. On average, 131 jobs were created per investment project. However, there was a big variation in the number of jobs created per project from year to year. In 2007, greenfield investments in the United States created 306 jobs per project; in 2008, 115 jobs per project; and in 2009, 192 jobs per project.

Figure 2-4: Jobs Analysis

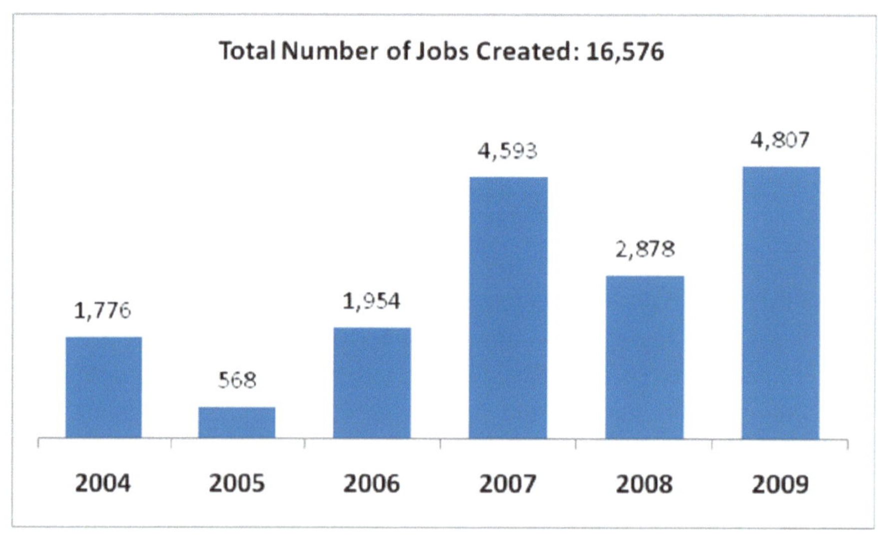

Source: Jobs data based on both actual and estimated values, provided by fDi Intelligence, Financial Times Ltd., U.K.

Finally, Table 2-2 highlights the 15 Indian companies that have created the most jobs in the United States based on their greenfield investments. The table shows that more than 60% of all jobs were created by 10 of the 90 Indian companies that made greenfield investments in the United States over the last six years.

Table 2-2: The Top 15 Indian Companies/Groups that Created the Most Jobs in the United States

Company	2004	2005	2006	2007	2008	2009	Total
Tata Group	175			1,000	82	1,228	2,485
Jindal Organization				1,895			1,895
Essar Group					700	1,000	1,700
Wipro				200		777	977
Welspun Group			143	550			693
Infosys Technologies	500				153		653
Reliance ADA						616	616
HCL Group					500	110	610
ICICI Bank	68				340		408
Classic Diamonds India			391				391
Mahindra & Mahindra						357	357
PSL				275			275
Bank of Baroda	204				68		272
Indage Group				252			252
Infotech Enterprises		242					242
Other Companies	829	326	1,420	421	1,035	719	4,750
Total	**1,776**	**568**	**1,954**	**4,593**	**2,878**	**4,807**	**16,576**

Source: Jobs data, based on both actual and estimated values, provided by fDi Intelligence, Financial Times Ltd., U.K.

Notes

The data on jobs created show actual/estimated numbers of direct jobs created by individual companies in the year of greenfield investment, based on data provided by fDi Markets, a unit of the *Financial Times* of U.K. However, when a company sets up a manufacturing plant, say, in Ohio in 2006, it may taken them two, three, or more years for the new plant to be fully operational and have the full employee strength.

The data shown here refer to only the entry investments in the United States. Companies typically make additional investments over time, with funds received from the parent company, capital raised in the U.S. or elsewhere, or reinvested profits. These subsequent investments are not shown in this report, though we do include such investments in the case studies presented here. Also not included are indirect jobs created by Indian companies through their investments in the United States.

Case Study: Essar Steel Makes the Impossible Possible in Minnesota

Essar Steel of India is setting up a vertically integrated steel plant on the Mesabi iron range in northeast Minnesota. To be completed by 2012, the project will cost $1.6 billion and the plant will have an annual capacity of 2.5 million tons of steel per annum when completed. It will be the first facility in North America to include iron ore mining, ore processing, direct reduction, and steelmaking on a single site. The projected permanent employee strength is 700, and up to 2,000 workers are being employed during the construction phase, 2008-2012.

Essar Steel Minnesota will use the latest and most environmentally sensitive technology and processes, utilizing natural gas and electricity to produce steel. Having all processes on one site will allow the company to minimize product movement and maximize energy savings. This, combined with the captive iron ore resource, will result in Essar Steel Minnesota being a low cost steel producer in North America.

The project broke ground on September 19, 2008, when state and local officials, including Minnesota Governor Tim Pawlenty, joined senior Essar executives for the groundbreaking ceremony at the project site near Nashwauk. (Read Governor Pawlenty's remarks on p2).

Minnesota Senator Tom Saxhuag[xvi] remarked on the merits of the project:

> *"Essar Steel Minnesota is an excellent example of the kind of economic development we want and need on the IronRange. The project not only will mine iron ore, it also will make steel – generating value-added benefits and creating high-tech jobs for our people. This is an example of how various institutions and hard-working people can get together to do a project that some thought was impossible."*

The Mayor of Nashwauk, Bill Hendricks, added, "Everybody in Nashwauk is so excited that this day has finally come. We know that it is a historic event and we couldn't be happier. We realize that this project will be a huge boost to the economy for NE Minnesota. We look forward to this joyous day of celebration."

At the groundbreaking ceremony, Essar Group Chairman Shashi Ruia, said:

"We are excited about starting this project. Today's groundbreaking is another step towards our goal of building a large presence in the steel sector in the Americas. We thank Governor Pawlenty and the local administration for lending their support to our IronRange project. Essar remains committed to North America with investments of over USD 4 billion in the region and currently employs more than 8,000 people here."

Essar Steel Minnesota is part of Essar Steel, a global producer of steel with a footprint covering India, Canada, United States, Middle East, and Asia. It is a fully integrated flat carbon steel manufacturer from iron ore to ready-to-market products.

Section 3. Mergers & Acquisitions by Indian Companies in the United States

> *"Not all emerging multinationals have the luxury of time to build a brand as Korea's Samsung and Chile's Concha y Toro have done. Chinese [and Indian] firms, in particular, appear anxious to prove themselves in the global marketplace even as foreign brands have begun to poach customers in their home market."*
>
> - Antoine van Agtmael, *The Emerging Markets Century: How a New Breed of World-Class Companies is Overtaking the World*, Free Press, 2007

It took Samsung two decades to achieve global brand leadership from scratch – painstakingly and expensively. However, many emerging market firms with global aspirations find such a route to success too long and too risky. In an era of accelerating globalization and technological change, they simply do not have the luxury of time to build their businesses and brands in foreign markets. One approach that has found favor with emerging market multinationals, flushed with cash from their huge domestic markets, is mergers and acquisitions – acquiring talent, technologies, markets, and brands outright.[xvii]

Merger & acquisition (M&A) has been a popular entry strategy for a large number of Indian firms in the six year period of this study. Our study of Indian firms' M&As is based on data on individual M&A transactions available from several published sources (FICCI and Ernst & Young studies, Virtus Global, and *Economic Times*), unpublished data received from Professor Jaya Prakash Pradhan of the Sardar Patel Institute of Economic & Social Research, Thompson SDC Database, our own research, and some company interviews. For details, please see the Methodology section.

Main Findings

This section summarizes M&A investment data over the last six years and offers insights into these investments by location, sector, and company as well as trends for investments, jobs, and projects over time. Please note that some information was unavailable and is, therefore, not included in our report. 239 Indian companies made 372 acquisitions in the U.S. during the period 2004 to 2009. Information on the deal value was available for only 267 of the 372 acquisitions completed during the last six years. Further, job creation/retention data were available for only 85 of the 372 acquisitions.

Indian Companies' M&As in the United States

Between January 2004 and December 2009, 239 Indian companies invested about $21 billion through 267 acquisitions in the United States. The value of these acquisitions was about four times the value of greenfield investments ($5 billion) made by Indian companies in the United States. Figure 3-1 highlights the major U.S. sectors in which Indian companies made acquisitions.

Figure 3-1: The Top Ten U.S. Sectors with Acquisitions from Indian Companies, 2004-2009

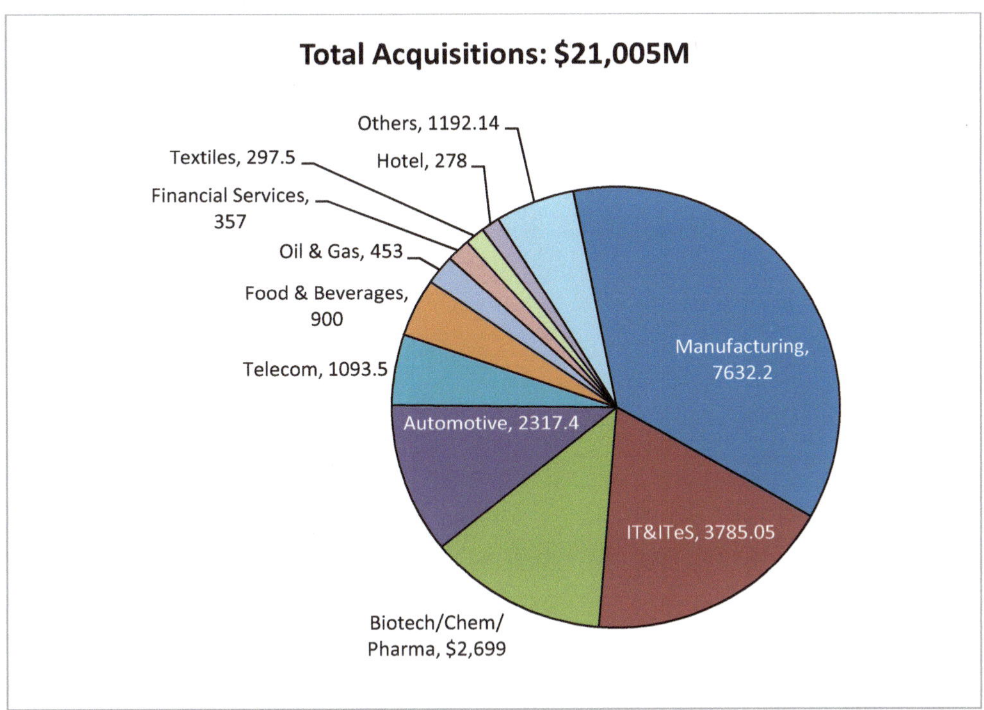

Source: Various sources; see Methodology

More than 80 percent of the $21 billion in M&A investments were in five sectors, Manufacturing; IT and ITeS (IT enabled Services); Biotechnology, Chemicals, and Pharmaceuticals; Automotive; and Telecom. It's noteworthy that manufacturing attracted the most investments by Indian companies, about twice as much as IT and ITeS for which Indian companies are well known.

Table 3-1 shows the Top Ten U.S. states in which these 267 acquisitions took place. In terms of value of investment, 75 percent of these transactions were in five states, Georgia, New Jersey, Michigan, California, and Texas. However, in terms of the number of investments, the top five recipient states were California, New York, New Jersey, Illinois, and Michigan (which tied with Texas for the fifth place). The average value per acquisition was $78.7 million.

Table 3-1: Top Ten U.S. States with Acquisitions from Indian Companies, 2004-2009

State Rank	State	Total Acquisition Value ($M)	Number of Acquisitions	Value Per Acquisition ($M)
1	Georgia	$6,283.5	9	$698.2
2	New Jersey	$2,874.8	33	$87.1
3	Michigan	$2,581.1	13	$198.6
4	California	$2,375.0	55	$43.2
5	Texas	$1,539.9	13	$118.5
6	Louisiana	$650.3	3	$216.8
7	New York	$641.3	23	$27.9
8	Maryland	$563.9	8	$70.5
9	Illinois	$486.5	17	$28.6
10	Connecticut	$353.0	4	$88.3
Total (Incl. State Not Specified)		**$21,004.6**	**267**	**$78.7**

Source: Various sources; see Methodology

Figure 3-2, shows the trend of acquisitions by year. On average, over the last six years, Indian companies acquired 45 companies a year in the United States.

Figure 3-2: Acquisition Trend Analysis

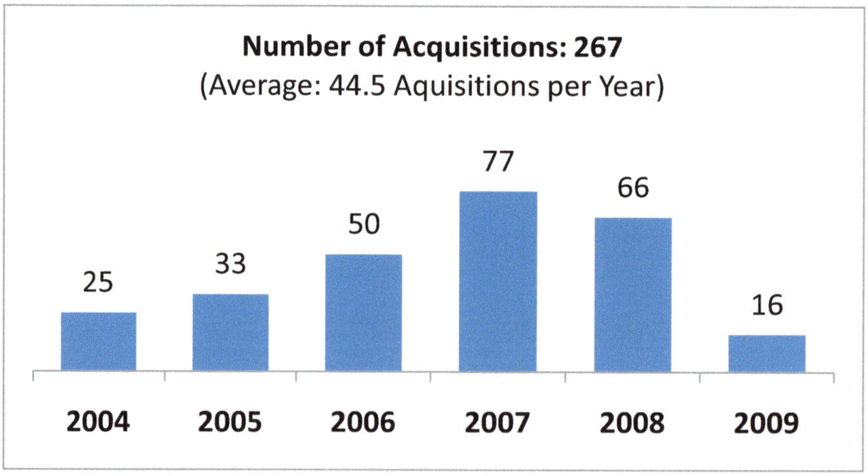

Source: Various sources; see Methodology

The number of acquisitions per year continued to increase from year-to-year until 2007. There was a 14% drop in the number of acquisitions in 2008, and an even more significant 75% drop between 2008 and 2009, as a result of the worldwide recession in those years.

In Figure 3-3, one can observe a similar trend for the deal value of the 267 acquisitions which averaged $3.5 billion a year. Here, deal value of acquisitions continued to increase from year-to-year until 2007, after which there was a major decrease in the average deal value (45% fall in 2008 and a further 94% fall in 2009). On average, each acquisition cost $78.7 million.

Figure 3-3: Acquisition Value Analysis

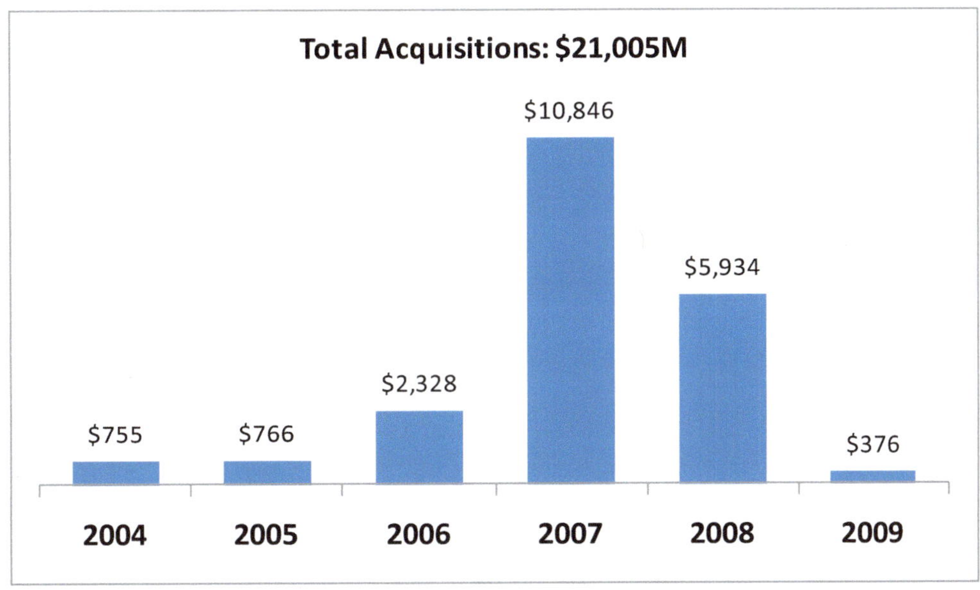

Source: Various sources; see Methodology

Jobs Created/Saved through Mergers and Acquisitions

As mentioned before, job creation/saving data was only available for 85 of 372 acquisitions completed over the last six years. Overall, these 85 acquisitions helped create or retain over 40,000 jobs in the United States. Therefore, we can infer that the actual number of workers employed by the 239 Indian companies that made 372 acquisitions in the U.S. during this time period will be much larger.

(Based on 2002 statistics available from the Bureau of Economic Analysis, U.S. affiliates of Indian companies employed 1,600 U.S. workers in 2002 and the number increased by 37.5% to 2,200 in 2003. Assuming the same rate of growth, the estimated number of U.S. workers by June 2009 should be 14,868. However, in 2009, the Tata Group alone had over 15,500 employees in 43 states and the District of Columbia.)

Table 3-2 provides information on the ten companies that have helped create/save about 30,000 jobs. The data addresses jobs created or saved during the last six years and does not include the number of employees the acquiring companies already had in their existing or greenfield operations in the United States.

Table 3-2: The Top 10 Indian Companies/Groups that Created/Saved the Most Jobs in the United States through M&A, 2004-2009

Acquirer	M&A Target	No. of Jobs Created/Saved
Cbay	Medquist	7,500
Firstsource Solutions	Several Companies	5,338
Aegis BPO	PeopleSupport	4,025
Hindalco	Novelis*	3,200
Tata Companies	Several Companies	2,822
HOV Services	BPO Lason	2,636
3i Infotech	Regulus, Innovative Business Solutions	1,875
Wipro	Infocrossing, Quantech Global	892
Sanmar	Matrix Metal Inc	877
Intelenet Global	Upstream	750
	Total	**29,915**

*U.S. and Canada

Source: Various sources

Penetration of Indian Investments in U.S. States

During the period January 2004 to December 2009, Indian companies made the highest number of acquisitions in California – 55 in all – or over 20% of the 267 acquisitions for which we have data on the amounts invested. The next three states in order of number of acquisitions are: New Jersey, New York, and Illinois. Investments in these four states account for 48% of the total number of acquisitions made by Indian companies during this period of time.

In terms of amount of money invested, five states received 75% of the total investments made by Indian companies' 267 acquisitions. These states are Georgia, New Jersey, Michigan, California, and Texas, in that order.

Over 30 Indian companies made acquisitions in at least 3 U.S. states each. The Tata Group has the greatest penetration in states, with presence in 43 states and the District of Columbia and over 15,500 employees. MedAssist, a Firstsource Solutions company, has a national presence with 37 regional offices in 19 states and over 4,500 employees. They support approximately 1,000 clients including some of the most respected healthcare providers in the nation.

A few other Indian companies with large U.S. presence are:

- Gitanjali Gems: Gitanjali Gems has a 97 percent stake in Samuels Jewelers Inc., which owns 97 retail stores in 18 states. And, Gitanjali's acquisition of Rogers Jewelers, which runs a chain of 46 retail stores in 11 states, further extended its U.S. presence.
- KC Management Group: KC Management Group, a CORE Projects & Technologies Ltd. company, currently provides services to school systems in ten states: California, Illinois, Minnesota, Florida, Georgia, South Carolina, Tennessee, Texas, Massachusetts, and Ohio.
- Styx Infosoft Pvt Ltd acquired a 49 percent stake in Citizens Financial Mortgage Inc., which has 290 employees in 45 branches spread across 16 states in the United States.

Case Study: Jain Irrigation Systems Ltd.

Established in 1987, Jain Irrigation Systems Ltd is a 5,082-employee environmentally conscious Indian company with operations in 110 countries. The company's mission statement reads, "Leave this world better than you found it." Its products aim to conserve nature's precious resources through substitution or value addition.

There is, of course, more to Jain Irrigation than *irrigation*. In addition to Drip and Sprinkler Irrigation Systems and Components the company manufactures PVC, Polyethylene & Polypropylene Piping Systems and Plastic Sheets. Other business lines include Dehydrated Onions and Vegetables, Processed Fruits, Tissue Culture, Hybrid & Grafted Plants, Greenhouses, Poly & Shade Houses, Bio-fertilizers, Solar Water Heating Systems, Solar Photovoltaic Appliances (Solar lighting systems), and Bio-Energy sources. The company also provides consulting services for project planning and implementation on topics like watersheds, wastelands, and crop selection and rotation.

The company's U.S. subsidiary, Jain (Americas), Inc., commenced operations in Columbus, Ohio in 1992. It served the sign, display and graphic arts industries with extruded Polycarbonate sheets and two types of PVC sheets that quickly gained acceptance by U.S. plastics distributors. By 2002, Jain (Americas) had entered the building materials industry by providing sheet stock and had introduced the Ex-cel® line of PVC products. Today Jain (Americas) also has over 150,000 square feet of manufacturing and warehousing space to serve the building and graphic arts industries with Free Foam.

Figure 3-4: Jain Americas NuCedar Mills Plant in Chicopee, MA

In 2006 and 2007, Jain Americas acquired four U.S. companies: Chapin Watermatics, NuCedar, Cascade, and Aquarius Brands. The acquisitions were made to access new market segments, get involved with new products, and to establish new marketing outlets for their irrigation products. One of the acquired companies was having financial difficulties and was actively seeking a buyer. The following table summarizes these acquisitions:

Table 3-3: Acquisitions by Jain Americas ($M)

U.S. Company Acquired	Segment	Location	Date of Acquisition	Initial & Subsequent Investments	Working Capital Loans	% Owner-ship
Chapin Watermatics	Micro Irrigation	New York	May-06	$6.81	$1.00	100%
NuCedar Mills Inc.	PVC Siding & Trim Boards	Mass.	Sep-06	$4.00	$5.13	80%
Cascade Specialties Inc.[1]	Onion Dehydration	Oregon	Jan-07	$7.82	$7.31	80%
Aquarius Brands[2]	Micro Irrigation	California	Feb-07	$15.15	$1.86	100%
Total				**$33.78**	**$15.30**	

1. Balance (20%) will be acquired by Dec-11

(Source: P3 on the Company's Investor Information section at: http://www.jains.com/Company/financial/annual%2009/Management%20Discussion%20n%20Analysis.pdf)

2. Renamed Jain Irrigation Inc.

The table above shows that Jain Americas has invested $33.8M in these acquisitions since 2006. Since the acquisitions, the U.S. employee base for these four companies has grown by

21 percent from 219 to 264. Additionally, Jain (Americas) Inc. has 15 employees in its U.S. headquarters. Only 4 of the 279 employees across all five entities are from India.

Jain (Americas) Inc. is the U.S. marketing, distribution, and investment arm for Jain Irrigation Systems Ltd. During the period April 2008 to March 2009, Jain (Americas) Inc. had sales of $23.36 million. The new acquisitions brought additional revenue of $62.9 million over the same fiscal year:

- Jain Irrigation Inc. (formerly Aquarius Brands and Chapin Watermatics): $46.75 million
- Cascade Specialties Inc.: $15.41 million
- NuCedar Mills Inc.: $ 0.74 million

Like any company, Jain Americas pays state and federal corporate taxes and payroll taxes. In 2008, the company paid $1.6 million in taxes. The following table shows three additional sources of impact, namely, investments in research and development (R&D), exports from the U.S., and the number of U.S. patents issued.

Table 3-4: Additional Sources of Impact ($M)

U.S. Company	Segment	Investment in R&D	Exports from the U.S.	No. of U.S. Patents Issued
Chapin Watermatics	Micro Irrigation	$0.14		
NuCedar Mills Inc.	PVC Siding & Trim Boards			2 Patents on manufacturing processes
Cascade Specialties Inc.	Onion Dehydration	$3.03	$7.10	
Aquarius Brands	Micro Irrigation	$3.88	$15.00	8 Patents for irrigation products processes & designs
Jain (Americas) Inc.	Plastic Sheets Marketing	$0.02		
Total		**$7.07**	**$22.10**	

Source: Jain Americas Inc.

In keeping with their mission, the Jain Americas companies support community initiatives like the California Water Alliance and the California Latino Water Coalition aimed at finding a comprehensive water solution for California. They also fund research at the Kansas State University. And, this year, NuCedar donated products to a community member in need through ABC's Extreme Makeover Home Edition.

Case Study: HCL Technologies

HCL Technologies is one of India's original IT start-ups and a pioneer in modern computing. Soon after Shiv Nader founded HCL in 1976, HCL became the first Indian computer manufacturer and established itself as a leader in computer hardware and operating systems in India. By the late 1980s, the company entered into a joint venture with Hewlett Packard and began exploring international markets.

Today, HCL Technologies is a $2.5 billion (as of December 31, 2009) leading global IT services company with 55,688 employees working in 26 countries with clients in the areas that impact and redefine the core of their businesses.

Its American subsidiary, HCL America, was established in 1989 and is headquartered in Sunnyvale, California. With more than 3,000 people across 21 offices in 15 states, HCL America accounts for 55.9% of HCL's total worldwide Consulting and IT Services revenues. HCL America is on a growth trajectory exemplified by its 34.2% year-over-year revenue growth in the quarter ending June 2008.

In 2005, HCL underwent radical transformation that led to a focus on "value centricity" and establishment of three services portfolios spanning a variety of industries including Financial Services, Manufacturing, Consumer Services, Public Services and Healthcare: IT Transformation Portfolio, Operations Transformation Portfolio, and the Technology Transformation Portfolio.

As part of this transformation, HCL pioneered the management concept of "Employee First, Customer Second" and empowered its employees to better serve its customers through fresh and innovative approaches. One of the program's initiatives involved hiring graduates from top U.S. schools such as the University of Michigan, Northwestern, NYU, Notre Dame, and Duke. Another initiative took advantage of customer engagements designed to overcome cultural and business nuances. Other concepts such as transformational engagements, outcome-based-pricing, and multi-service delivery also became cornerstones of HCL's strategy.

HCL's innovative thinking and management style raised the company's profile in the United States and made it the subject of classroom discussion, following the publication of a case study on HCL by the Harvard Business School in 2007. The *Fortune* magazine featured HCL's management as the 'world's most innovative management' in April 2006 and *Business Week*, *USA Today*, and *Investor's Business Daily* have also recognized the company's unique management approach.

In 2009, HCL was featured in the prestigious FinTech Top 25 Enterprise Technology Companies for the first time. Shiv Nadar, the founder, Chairman and Chief Strategy Officer, has been conferred the 'CNBC Asia Business Leader Award 2009 for Corporate Social Responsibility' as well as the 'Asia Viewers' Choice Award.' He was also presented with CNBC's 'India Business Leader Award' for 2009 by the CNBC Asia's International Jury.

In recent years, HCL America has built significant strategic partnerships with several American industry giants including Boeing, CISCO, Oracle, Jones New York, and Merck & Co. Since 2004, the company has invested more than $80 million in U.S. companies to acquire new capabilities and create more value in key industries and sub-industries.

Aalayance. HCL invested $0.45million in 2003 and $1.9 million in 2004 to acquire a 66 percent stake in California-based Aalayance, renamed HCL EAI Services Inc. in 2004. HCL invested an additional $3.49 million in HCL EAI Services Inc. in 2007, giving it a 100 percent ownership of HCL EAI. HCL EAI Services, Inc. provides enterprise application integration services to healthcare, retail, telecommunication, and wireless community markets internationally. It offers outsourcing services in the areas of application development, migration, re-engineering, renovation, and system software.

Capital Stream. HCL acquired the Washington-based Capital Stream for $40 million in 2008, which provided it a number of synergies, benefits, and opportunities, including:

- the addition of a focused product portfolio to HCL's multi-service capability to enable it to provide commercial banks and other financial institutions comprehensive end-to-end solutions globally, with significantly reduced implementation time;
- the offerings from Capital Stream that complement HCL's lending technology capabilities in financial services.

Control Point Systems. HCL acquired the New Jersey-based Control Point Systems for $20.8 million in 2008. Control Point has four delivery centers in the U.S. with over 200 professionals who provide voice, data, and wireless telecommunications expense management (TEM) services. The acquisition improved HCL's ability to provide end-to-end BPO (business process outsourcing) services in the TEM space and allowed the company to diversify into newer geographic and product markets like utilities and freight.

Data Center. HCL completed the acquisition of its first U.S.-based data center, a 35,000-square-foot facility in New Jersey in 2009. HCL took over this data center's staff and operations from a Fortune 500 enterprise in October 2008 and has already invested more than $15 million in this facility in upgrades to support eco-friendly technologies, virtualization, cloud computing, business continuity, and mainframe management services. HCL is further upgrading the facility to a Tier III equivalent data center by deploying best-of-breed eco-friendly technologies from leading solution/technology vendors and acquiring world-class certifications. The company plans to hire more than 100 local U.S. workers for this state-of-the-art facility.

In addition to these acquisitions, HCL America is continuing to grow its U.S. operations organically. It recently announced plans to open a delivery center in Wake County, North Carolina. The company plans to invest $3.2 million and hire more than 500 employees over the next five years at the new delivery center, thanks in part to a North Carolina state Job Development Investment Grant awarded to the company. The new jobs will focus on software development and infrastructure services.

Case Study: Ranbaxy Laboratories Ltd.

India's largest pharmaceutical company, Ranbaxy had global sales of $1.519 billion in 2009, of which the United States healthcare market accounted for $397 million. The company has presence in 46 countries, with products serving customers in 125 countries, and derives approximately 75 percent of its revenues from outside India. While primarily marketing generic product formulations in the U.S. market, Ranbaxy has 16 branded products and has established presence in both prescription and over-the-counter drugs for both sectors.

Ranbaxy entered the United States in 1994 with an office in Raleigh, NC, and relocated to, New Jersey in 1998. The company follows a localization strategy in the markets where it does business. According to CEO and Managing Director Atul Sobti, "When entering the U.S. market, Ranbaxy hired local Americans in the community with pharmaceutical expertise and looked to them as mentors who knew the markets and were able to provide organizational guidance."

Ranbaxy acquired manufacturing facilities in New Jersey in 1995 with an investment of around $8 million. Subsequently, the company expanded capabilities and capacities by enlarging and acquiring facilities that today occupy more than 250,000 sq. ft. in New Jersey in 2009 from 40,000 sq. ft. in 1995. During this time period, a new manufacturing facility for the manufacture of liquid product formulations in New York State was added, along with investment in a U.S. distribution facility located in the State of Florida. Over the years, the company invested an aggregate total in excess of $100 million in these facilities.

In the United States, the company has operations in New Jersey (administrative headquarters for North America plus manufacturing), New York (manufacturing), and Florida (distribution center). Presently Ranbaxy's U.S. operations have a total of 659 employees, of which 596 are in New Jersey, 13 in New York, and 50 in Florida. In 2008, Ranbaxy paid $3 million in payroll taxes to these three states.

Ranbaxy performs research and development in its R&D center in India, which has more than 1,400 researchers. Since establishing US operations, Ranbaxy has filed over 200 drug molecule applications with U.S. Food and Drug Administration and has received 140+ approvals so far; 80+ applications pending approval.

Ranbaxy contributes to the communities and countries where it does business and has been recognized for its contributions. For instance, the White House recognized Ranbaxy America for its help during Katrina. Ranbaxy has also been at the forefront to provide relief to AIDS patients on a global basis through its involvement with PEPFAR, OGAC, and the United Nations. Most recently, contributions were made through U.S.-based relief organizations providing aid to the devastation experienced in Haiti in 2010. In New Jersey, Ranbaxy America contributes to civic organizations such as the Plainsboro Public Library and local charities.

Daiichi Sankyo Co. Ltd. of Japan acquired a significant stake in Ranbaxy Laboratories Ltd. in June 2008 to create an entity ranked among the Top 20 global pharmaceutical companies.

Case Study: Firstsource Solutions Limited

Firstsource, a global provider of business process management services, works across the banking and financial services, telecommunications, media, and healthcare industries. The company supports the complete customer lifecycle, including customer acquisition, customer care, billing and collections, transaction processing, and business research and analytics. Firstsource's *rightshoring* approach utilizes a global delivery model with 42 world class centers and over 24,000 employees across India, the U.S., U.K., and the Philippines. Firstsource has been ranked among the world's Top 100 companies by CIO magazine for innovative uses of IT.

In the United States, Firstsource has delivery centers in New York, Kansas, Kentucky, Illinois, Nevada, Utah, and Colorado, and has invested more than $400 million in four U.S. companies since 2004. These are:

Pipal Research, acquired for $3.9 million in 2004. Pipal is engaged in providing business research services to companies in the BFSI industry.

Account Solution Group, acquired for $42.5 million in 2004. New York-based ASG's 500 U.S. employees provide BPO services in the collective services segment.

BPM Inc., acquired for $30 million in 2007, BPM Inc is a 300-employee Delaware-based healthcare claims outsourcing company. The acquisition includes BPM Inc.'s two wholly owned operating subsidiaries, MedPlans 2000 Inc. and MedPlans Partners.

MedAssist Holdings, acquired for $330 million in 2007. MedAssist, headquartered in Louisville, Kentucky has 4,500 employees in 37 locations and is a pan-American provider of revenue cycle management services to the healthcare industry. In 2009, MedAssist was ranked second among US Healthcare vendors by KLAS for Extended Business Office services.

Case Study: Rolta

Rolta, headquartered in Mumbai, employs about 5,000 professionals with a countrywide infrastructure and international subsidiaries across the globe. Forbes Global has ranked Rolta amongst the "Best 200 under a Billion" for four of the last six years. Rolta has been included in the S&P Global Challengers List™ 2008, by Standard & Poor's. This list identifies 300 mid-size companies worldwide that have a total market capitalization between US$ 1 & 5 billion and have shown the highest growth characteristics along dimensions encompassing intrinsic and extrinsic growth.

Rolta is a global market leader and IT solution provider in the Geospatial, Defense, Homeland Security, Government, Utilities & Communications, Transportation, Process & Power, and Enterprise IT sectors. The company has subsidiaries in the U.S., U.A.E., Saudi Arabia, U.K. and France. Over the years, the company has successfully executed multi-million dollar contracts across a broad spectrum of industries in over 40 countries.

Figure 3-5: Rolta Headquarters in the U.S.

Rolta invests in vertical solutions that are targeted in various industries to improve productivity. As a part of its systematic and aggressive growth plans, Rolta has adopted a clear acquisition strategy of taking over companies that provide a synergetic mix of Technology and IPR, enabling Rolta to move up the value chain for addressing complementary markets.

Rolta's entry into the U.S. was through a greenfield investment of $36 million in 1992. The investment funded the establishment of Rolta International Inc. in Georgia. In 2008, Rolta acquired three US companies in Chicago for $61.3 million – TUSC Inc., WhittmanHart Consulting Services, and Piocon Technologies Inc. One of the acquired companies was financially stressed and Rolta's acquisition of the company helped retain 58 jobs.

TUSC provides IT consultancy in the area of ERP applications as well as Database and Business Intelligence solutions, based on Oracle technologies.

With WhittmanHart Consulting, Rolta can now offer a more complete range of business solutions and consulting services, such as EPM and risk management, especially to its GIS/geospatial and engineering clients. At the same time, Rolta can also leverage the WhittmanHart Consulting customer base by offering its complementary solution suite.

Finally, the acquisition of Piocon Technologies has provided Rolta with a template-based solution to address critical operational needs of refineries in the oil and gas sector.

Rolta currently has 300 employees in the United States. The company also plans to invest $3.5 million annually in research and development activities in the United States.

Case Study: Polaris Software

Founded in 1993 and publicly-listed, Polaris Software is one of the world's most sophisticated banking and insurance software company. Polaris is the chosen outsourcing partner for 10 of the top 15 global banks and 6 of the top 10 global insurance companies. Polaris offers comprehensive solutions for core banking, corporate banking, wealth & asset management and insurance. Over the last two decades, Polaris has implemented its solutions and services in 200 of the world's largest financial institutions. Polaris Software is also recognized by the world's top analysts (Forrester and Gartner) as global leaders in banking and insurance software. Polaris has 10,500 associates including 750 domain experts in 23 international offices and four global development centers.

Polaris operates in the United States through its four offices in California, Illinois, and New Jersey; and its subsidiary Optimus Global Services Limited in Delaware. Polaris invested $2 million in February 1999 to set up a branch office in Iselin, NJ and $50,000 in May 2007 to acquire Optimus. It started with 200 employees in New Jersey in 1999 and now has 606 employees in New Jersey and 15 employees in Pennsylvania.

Polaris's most recent acquisition in the U.S. was SEEC Inc. in October 2008 for $7.5 million. SEEC is an innovative and well respected worldwide Service-Oriented-Architecture-based insurance solution provider.

Case Study: Indegene Life Systems Pvt. Ltd.

Indegene's mission is to enhance commercialization and marketing success of life science companies through their ability to understand, analyze, and apply knowledge of science and clinical practice. It's a preferred global partner to more than fifteen of the top twenty pharmaceutical companies in the world and has presence in the United States, United Kingdom, Singapore, Malaysia, Indonesia, and Australia. In 2005 and 2006, Indegene acquired two failing companies, Medsn Inc. and MedCases LLC, reviving them both in the following years.

Medsn Inc. is a New Jersey-based venture capital-funded company with an initial investment of $39 million and it employed 40 employees. Medsn was operating at a loss for seven years and was on the brink of bankruptcy in 2005 at the time Indegene acquired it for $15.5 million in September. Since then Indegene has turned the company around and has been able to save approximately 15 of the existing high paying jobs. Medsn Inc. has led the development of a number of products based on pre-existing technology for Learning Management Systems. It has also re-launched many of its pre-existing products and solutions, with exports to emerging markets across Asia and Africa.

MedCases LLC, based in Princeton, New Jersey, was also acquired when it was on the verge of bankruptcy. When Indegene acquired MedCases for $0.8 million in September 2006, the company had no employees. Since the acquisition, the operation has become profitable and currently has five employees. MedCases has been running a unique operation (with Johns Hopkins University) to educate physicians across Africa using MedCases products and technology.

Case Study: Infotech Enterprises Group

Infotech Enterprises Group, founded in 1991, is a $200 million Global IT services company with over 7,600 employees specializing in engineering services, geographic information systems (GIS), and IT services. It provides services to a wide range of industries, including Aerospace, Automotive, Energy, Government, HiTech Consumer & Medical Devices, Marine, Rail, Retail, Telecom, and Utilities.

Infotech has a distinctive business model, "offshore services, onshore responsibility." It combines extensive software development capability based in India with global delivery through offices in the U.S., U.K., Germany, Australia, and the Netherlands that provide local customer interface and project management. It operates from 27 global locations, and has 7 development centers.

Since 1999, Infotech has made several investments in the United States, first establishing Infotech Enterprises America Inc. in 1999 through a greenfield investment of $150,000 in East Hartford, Connecticut. Subsequently, they made investments totaling $2.85 million for various expansions. And, in May 2005, Infotech inaugurated a geospatial production facility in Frostburg, Maryland.

Infotech made two acquisitions during the study period – Vargis, a GIS company, for $2.95 million in January 2004, and Time To Market (TTM), a California-based provider of ASIC design and embedded software solutions in September 2008 for $6 million. TTM with 40 engineers based in San Jose, California, became part of the newly created Hitech vertical at Infotech to focus on U.S. markets and to leverage its recent entry into Japan.

Infotech Enterprises America Inc. currently has 396 employees, with revenues of $74 million in FY 2008-09. The company paid $2.4 million in Federal, $60,000 in State, and $1.8 million in payroll taxes in 2008.

Section 4. A Splendid Exchange[1]

How the United States and India both Benefit from Trade

> *"Trade raises the general wage level by expanding the opportunity for Americans to work in sectors where productivity and pay exceed the average. Because of comparative advantage, American workers tend to be most productive in those sectors that are most capital intensive – those that require large investments in physical and human capital and intellectual property... Trade has delivered better jobs for American workers. Most of the net new jobs created in the past decade pay more than the average manufacturing job."*
>
> - Daniel Griswold, *Mad About Trade: Why Main Street America Should Embrace Globalization,* Cato Institute, 2009

In his fascinating book, *A Splendid Exchange: How Trade Shaped the World*, William Bernstein shows how trade has been a key element in the wealth of nations for millennia. As humans, we want new, cheaper, and better goods and services, and trade makes it possible – and, in the process, unites us beyond geographies, languages, cultures, and politics. The history of trade between America and India has indeed been a splendid exchange!

In the 1700s, America traded more with India than with all of Europe combined. Today, India is America's 17th largest export market.

Table 4-1shows that trade between the U.S. and India tripled over the five-year period, 2004-2008, benefiting both the United States and India. In the last six years (2004-2009), U.S. exports to India have increased by 269 percent. During the same period, India's exports to the United States grew by 136 percent.

[1] With apologies to William Bernstein, author of *A Splendid Exchange: How Trade Shaped the World,* Grove Press, New York, 2008

Table 4-1: U.S.-India Merchandise Trade, 2004, 2008 and 2009

Item	2004	2008	2009	CAGR* 2004-2008	CAGR* 2004-2009	% Overall Increase 2004-2008	% Overall Increase 2004-2009
Exports to India ($M)	6,109	17,682	16,462	30.43%	21.93%	289.43%	269.46%
Imports from India ($M)	15,572	25,704	21,176	13.35%	6.34%	165.07%	135.99%
Total U.S.-India Trade ($M)	**21,681**	**43,386**	**37,639**	**18.94%**	**11.66%**	**200.11%**	**173.60%**

* CAGR: Compounded Annual Growth Rate

Source: http://tse.export.gov/

U.S. Merchandise Exports to India

The United States exports to India high-technology products such as nuclear reactors, aircraft, electrical machinery, optic and surgical instruments, chemicals, plastics, pharmaceuticals, vehicles, and railway stock and traffic signal equipment, as well as natural pearls and precious stones, fertilizers, and iron and steel (Table 4-2), most of which pay much above-average employee wages. As the table shows, U.S. exports to India grew by a compounded annual growth rate of over 30% during 2004-2008, with spectacular increases for several industries. (The table excludes agricultural, mining, and services exports to India, which have their own implications for job creation in the United States).

By contrast, the Top 10 products the United States imports from India are: natural pearls and precious stones, pharmaceuticals, organic chemicals, apparel and accessories, needlecraft sets, electrical machinery, articles of iron and steel, nuclear reactors and machinery, and carpets. This is because of the comparative advantages India has in producing such, often low value-added, products, which go to lower the cost of living in the United States.

In fact, in a 2009 op-ed article in the *Hindustan Times*, Dr. Amit Mitra, Secretary-General of the Federation of Indian Chambers of Commerce & Industry, recommended an "ideal swap", whereby India should offer its huge market in exchange for technology and knowledge from the United States.[xviii]

Table 4-2: U.S. Merchandise Exports to India by Industry, 2004, 2008, and 2009

Top Ten Industries	U.S. Exports to India ($000)			CAGR 2004-2008	CAGR 2004-2009
	2004	2008	2009		
71--NAT ETC PEARLS, PREC ETC STONES, PR MET ETC; COIN	582,563	2,545,538	2,339,271	44.58%	32.05%
84--NUCLEAR REACTORS, BOILERS, MACHINERY ETC.; PARTS	1,148,051	2,322,424	2,325,100	19.26%	15.16%
88--AIRCRAFT, SPACECRAFT, AND PARTS THEREOF	482,749	1,849,480	2,254,144	39.90%	36.10%
85--ELECTRIC MACHINERY ETC; SOUND EQUIP; TV EQUIP; PTS	883,468	1,325,855	1,301,324	10.68%	8.05%
31—FERTILIZERS	118,701	2,787,348	1,157,693	120.13%	57.70%
27--MINERAL FUEL, OIL ETC.; BITUMIN SUBST; MINERAL WAX	313,696	884,550	959,775	29.58%	25.06%
90--OPTIC, PHOTO ETC, MEDIC OR SURGICAL INSTRMENTS ETC	461,524	917,004	920,479	18.73%	14.81%
72--IRON AND STEEL	158,247	572,120	643,007	37.89%	32.37%
29--ORGANIC CHEMICALS	470,526	589,663	641,764	5.80%	6.40%
39--PLASTICS AND ARTICLES THEREOF	157,729	499,755	637,031	33.42%	32.21%
Some Other High-Tech Industries					
38--MISCELLANEOUS CHEMICAL PRODUCTS	234,986	369,907	413,240	12.01%	11.95%
28--INORG CHEM; PREC & RARE-EARTH MET & RADIOACT COMP	35,999	366,066	209,916	78.57%	42.28%
87--VEHICLES, EXCEPT RAILWAY OR TRAMWAY, AND PARTS ETC	41,698	133,302	158,950	33.72%	30.69%
30--PHARMACEUTICAL PRODUCTS	27,650	87,422	126,405	33.35%	35.52%
86--RAILWAY OR TRAMWAY STOCK ETC; TRAFFIC SIGNAL EQ	16,938	31,148	51,788	16.45%	25.05%
Total Exports to India (All Industries)	**6,109,357**	**17,682,085**	**16,462,437**	**30.43%**	**21.93%**

Source: http://tse.export.gov/

In 2009, India was United States' 17th largest goods export market, and 15th largest supplier of goods imported into the United States. Goods exports to India account for 1.6 percent of U.S. exports worldwide, up from 1.4 percent in 2008, and from 0.5 percent in 1994 (the year WTO was founded).

United States exports to India grew by a *compounded annual growth rate* (CAGR) of 22% during the last six years, 2004-2009, and by over 30% during 2004-2008; exports suffered a decline due to the worldwide recession in 2008-2009. America's exports to India have been growing at a much faster rate than exports to practically all developed and developing nations (Table 4-3).

Table 4-3: Compounded Annual Growth Rates of U.S. Exports to Selected Developed and Developing Countries, 2004, 2008, and 2009

Country	U.S. Exports ($000)			CAGR 2004-2008	CAGR 2004-2009
	2004	2008	2009		
World Total	**814,874,654**	**1,287,441,997**	**1,056,931,976**	**12.11%**	**5.34%**
Canada	189,879,866	261,149,834	204,728,094	8.29%	1.52%
Mexico	110,731,285	151,220,056	128,997,679	8.10%	3.10%
China	34,427,772	69,732,838	69,576,048	19.30%	15.11%
Japan	53,568,694	65,141,753	51,179,644	5.01%	-0.91%
U.K.	35,901,658	53,599,070	45,713,722	10.54%	4.95%
Germany	31,415,882	54,505,256	43,298,596	14.77%	6.63%
South Korea	26,186,736	34,668,671	28,639,972	7.27%	1.81%
France	20,917,747	28,840,097	26,522,336	8.36%	4.86%
Brazil	13,886,423	32,298,655	26,175,324	23.49%	13.52%
India	**6,109,357**	**17,682,085**	**16,462,437**	**30.43%**	**21.93%**
Italy	10,684,740	15,460,836	12,232,636	9.68%	2.74%
Chile	3,605,984	11,857,444	9,365,333	34.66%	21.03%
Russian Fed.	2,960,997	9,334,582	5,382,838	33.25%	12.70%

Source: http://tse.export.gov/

Even from 2007 to 2008, U.S. merchandise exports to India grew by over 18%, when the world was experiencing a huge recession. According to Mark Zandi, chief economist at Moody's Economy.com, *"Exports have suddenly become a key source of growth at a time when the economy is looking for any growth it can get."*

Exports and Jobs

According to the U.S. Department of Commerce, in 2006, total manufactured exports from the United States accounted for 4.3 percent of all civilian employment in the U.S. In terms of jobs, U.S. worldwide manufactured exports in 2006 were linked to 2.6 million manufacturing and 3.4 million non-manufacturing jobs in the United States.[xix] (*Jobs linked to non-manufactured exports, such as agricultural and mineral products, and to services exports, are additional*).

United States' merchandise exports to India were linked to over 96,000 manufacturing and non-manufacturing jobs in the U.S. in 2009. Table 4-4 shows the total numbers of U.S. jobs linked to merchandise exports to India for the last six years. As indicated earlier, these numbers do not include U.S. jobs linked to exports of agricultural and mineral products as well as services to India. For instance, the United States exported $9.4 billion worth of services to India in 2007, compared to merchandise exports of $15 billion. Services exports to India must also account for tens of thousands of even higher value jobs in the United States.

Table 4-4: No. of U.S. Jobs Linked to U.S. Merchandise Exports to India, 2004-2009

	2004	2005	2006	2007	2008	2009
Total Exports ($M)	$6,109	$7,919	$9,674	$14,969	$17,682	$16,462
No. of U.S. Jobs Linked to Exports to India (Estimate)	33,961	44,018	53,774	83,210	98,292	96,026

Source: No. of jobs linked to manufactured exports to India estimated based on:
http://www.trade.gov/td/industry/otea/jobs/Reports/2006/jobs_by_state.html
(See the Methodology Appendix for more details)

Table 4-5 has information on the 25 U.S. states with the highest numbers of jobs linked to exports to India in 2009. It includes jobs in both manufacturing and non-manufacturing occupations linked to manufactured exports (and does not include non-manufactured exports, such as agricultural and mineral products, and services).

The Top 10 states, in terms of the number of jobs related to exports to India, are: California, Washington, Texas, Illinois, New York, Utah, Pennsylvania, South Carolina, Florida, and Georgia.

Table 4-5: The Top 25 States – Numbers of Jobs Linked to Manufactured Exports from Individual U.S. States to India in 2009

State	2009 Manufactured Exports ($M)	# Jobs Related to Exports (Estimate)
California	2,182	11,812
Texas	1,949	7,490
Washington	1,844	11,159
New York	1,515	5,333
Florida	1,051	3,494
Illinois	769	5,438
Louisiana	701	2,647
Utah	650	4,040
Pennsylvania	439	3,698
Georgia	420	3,478
New Jersey	405	1,943
Ohio	380	3,167
South Carolina	318	3,506
Massachusetts	306	2,139
Virginia	284	1,990
Maryland	233	1,229
Wisconsin	210	2,136
West Virginia	208	1,492
Indiana	192	1,631
North Carolina	187	1,641
Michigan	172	1,032
Tennessee	164	1,056
Alabama	161	1,297
Arkansas	158	1,942
Minnesota	148	1191
Total U.S. (Including Others)	**16,462**	**96,026**

Sources: Exports http://tse.export.gov/

No. of jobs linked to manufactured exports to India estimated based on:
http://www.trade.gov/td/industry/otea/jobs/Reports/2006/jobs_by_state.html
(See the Methodology Appendix for more details)

The Importance of India as an Export Market to Different States

The importance of India as an export destination varies from state to state. The following table shows the fifteen U.S. states with the highest percentage of their exports going to India.

Table 4-6: Share of India in Total State Merchandise Exports, 2009

State	Exports to India, 2009 ($M)	Total U.S. Exports, 2009 ($M)	India as % of Total U.S. Exports
Utah	650	10,337	6.28%
West Virginia	208	4,822	4.32%
Washington	1,844	51,739	3.56%
Arkansas	158	5,267	3.01%
New York	1,515	57,321	2.64%
Maryland	233	9,229	2.52%
Rhode Island	37	1,495	2.49%
Florida	1051	46,920	2.24%
Louisiana	701	32,715	2.14%
Mississippi	122	6,308	1.93%
South Carolina	318	16,516	1.93%
Virginia	284	15,045	1.89%
Illinois	769	41,514	1.85%
California	2182	120,142	1.82%
North Dakota	39	2,178	1.81%
Total - U.S.	**16,462**	**1,056,932**	**1.56%**

Source: http://tse.export.gov/

President Obama's State of the Union address on January 27, 2010 presented his policy solutions for resolving Americans' Number 1 concern – the economy and jobs. On the jobs front, he said that the United States will double its exports over the next five years, creating two million new jobs in the economy.

America's fastest growing export markets are the emerging markets of China, India, and Brazil. Of these three big export markets, U.S. merchandise exports grew the fastest to India over the last six years – by a compounded growth rate of over 22 percent per year – and almost 100,000 jobs were linked to manufactured exports to India in 2009. With India's penchant for all things American, and with the U.S.-India civilian nuclear agreement in hand, U.S. exports to India are likely to grow even faster in the coming years – creating even more jobs in the United States.

Section 5. Immigrant Entrepreneurs, Professionals, and Students from India

Give me your tired, your poor,
Your huddled masses yearning to breathe free,
The wretched refuse of your teeming shore.
Send these, the homeless, tempest-tossed to me,
I lift my lamp beside the golden door!

- Emma Lazarus, The New Colossus, 1883

When Emma Lazarus wrote the sonnet, The New Colossus, from which these famous lines were taken, she was referring to large numbers of European immigrants fleeing persecution and destitution in their native lands in the late 1800s – hoping for a better life in America, the land of opportunity. Many of them went on to become successful entrepreneurs, industrialists, scholars, scientists, and artists, making America what it is today.[xx]

Immigrants, and other professionals and students from India, who came to the United States in the last several decades, also seeking opportunity, however, do not fit the *huddled masses* connotation. They are often highly educated individuals bringing valuable skills, and they have been making a mark on American economy and society in many ways. However, the process known as "brain drain" has begun to reverse to some extent in the last decade.[xxi]

This section highlights the contributions of immigrant entrepreneurs, professionals, and students from India to the U.S. economy and society. Given the wide variety of pursuits they have followed, we have chosen to focus only on the contributions of these three sets of people of Indian origin in the United States.

Who are the Indian Americans

The Asian Indian[xxii] population in America, according to the American Community Survey of the U.S. Census Bureau, was 2.57 million in 2007, less than one percent of the U.S. population. They are the third largest Asian American ethnic group in the United States, after Chinese Americans and Filipino Americans. They are the most educated and have the highest income, compared to all other ethnic groups. The 2005 American Community Survey reported their median household income at $71,932, compared to the median household income of $46,242 for the total U.S. population. About 70 percent of the Indian Americans have a bachelor's degree or higher, almost three times the national average of 27 percent. Sixty-one percent of the Indian Americans are in management, professional, and related occupations compared to 34 percent for the total population. And, 19 percent of Indian Americans work in "professional, scientific, and management, and administrative and waste management services" industries compared to 10% for the United States population.[xxiii]

Immigrant Entrepreneurs from India

According to the Survey of Business Owners by the U.S. Census Bureau, there were 231,000 businesses owned by Indian Americans in 2002, which employed 615,000 workers and had revenues of over $89 billion. (The Census Bureau conducts the survey every five years, and the results of the 2007 survey are to become available starting in mid-2010).

Given their high educational, technical, and professional backgrounds, it is only to be expected that Indian Americans' contributions to the American economy and society are also much above average, as the following discussion shows.

High-tech Entrepreneurs. A 2007 joint Duke University-UC Berkeley study by Vivek Wadhwa and others found that Indian immigrants had founded more engineering and technology companies during 1995-2005 than immigrants from Britain, China, Japan, and Taiwan combined. [xxiv] Of all immigrant-founded companies, 26 percent had Indian founders. Figure 5-1 and Figure 5-2 show the states and the industries where immigrant Indian entrepreneurs had founded companies during the 1995-2005 decade (based on Wadhwa et al, 2007). The bulk of the companies they founded were in high-tech industries.

These results are not surprising given that immigrants tend to possess greater entrepreneurial capacity, particularly in technical fields – the finding of a 2007 National Venture Capital Association (NVCA) study, "American Made: The Impact of Immigrant Entrepreneurs and Professionals on U.S. Competitiveness."[xxv] According to the study, 25 percent of U.S. public venture capital-backed corporations were started by immigrants over the last fifteen years. Immigrant-founded venture-backed companies are concentrated in cutting-edge sectors, including high-tech manufacturing, information technology, and life sciences. The study also found that 40 percent of U.S. publicly traded venture-backed companies in high-technology manufacturing were started by immigrants.

Over half of the employment generated by U.S. public venture-backed high-tech manufacturers came from immigrant-founded companies. These companies pay high salaries to white collar American workers in professional positions. The NVCA survey also found that almost two-thirds of the immigrant founders of privately held venture-backed companies have started or intend to start more companies in the United States, thereby creating more jobs.

> *"The story is not new. Immigrants were founders of such corporations as Dow Chemical, DuPont, Pfizer, Proctor & Gamble and Carnegie (later U.S.) Steel. And not just yesteryear: Immigrants founded Google, Yahoo, Intel, PayPal and YouTube. Since 1995, they've formed more than half of new Silicon Valley firms, driving one of the world's hottest economies."*
>
> \- Neal Peirce, The Washington Post,

While immigrant founders in venture-backed public companies came from across the globe, India was the most common place of birth for foreign-born founders in the NVCA survey, followed by U.K., China, Iran, and France

Figure 5-1: Engineering and Technology Companies Founded by Immigrants from India

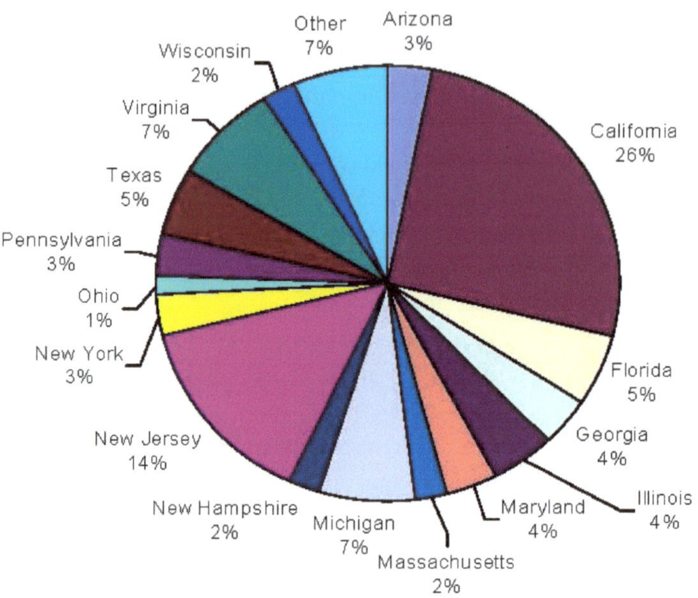

Figure 5-2: Industries in Which Immigrants from India Founded Companies

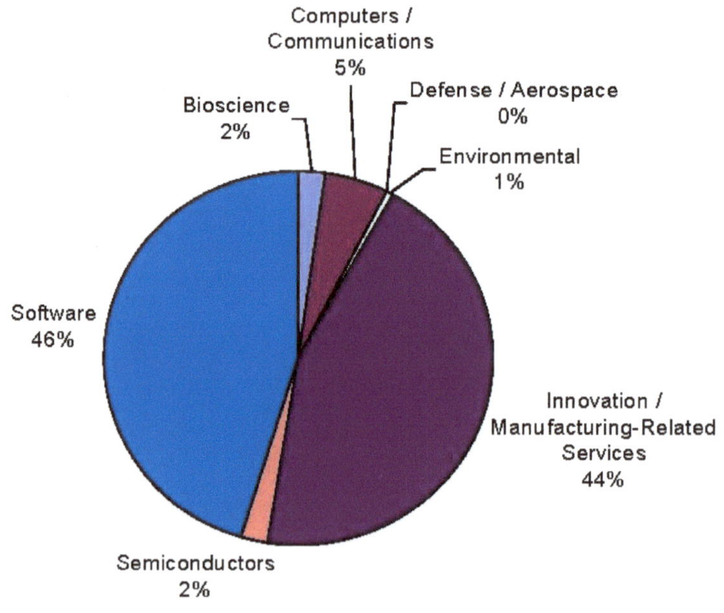

Source for Both Charts: Wadhwa et al, 2007

Table 5-1: Select Immigrant-Entrepreneurs from India and the Companies they Founded

Company	Founder/Cofounder (c)	State	Sales ($M)	Employees
Akamai	Preetish Nijhawan (c)	MA	859.8	1,750
Art Technology Group	Jeet Singh	MA	179.38	545
Bose Corporation	Amar Bose	MA	NA	8,000
Cirrus Logic	Suhas Patil (c)	TX	220.99	505
CyberMedia	Unni Warrier	CA	71.2	257
i2 Technologies Inc.	Sanjiv Sidhu	TX	256	1,280
iGate	Sunil Wadhwani (c)	CA	193.1	6,910
InfoGROUP Inc.	Vinod Gupta	NE	$500	3,146
Infospace	Naveen Jain	WA	207.65	157
Juniper Networks	Pradeep Sindhu	CA	3,320	7,231
Kanbay International Inc.	Dileep Nath (c)	IL	230.5	6,900
PortalPlayer Inc.	Sanjeev Kumar	CA	NA	201-500
Qlogic Corporaion	H. K. Desai	CA	549.07	1,038
SanDisk	Sanjay Mehrotra (c)	CA	3,570	3,267
Scandent Group	Ramesh Vangal	NJ	NA	3,000
SonicWall Inc.	Sreekanth Ravi	CA	200.57	819
Sun Microsystems	Vinod Khosla (c)	CA	11,450	29,000
Sycamore Networks	Desh Deshpande	MA	67.4	405
Synaptic Digital Inc	Shobha Purushothaman (c)	NY	NA	117
Syntel	Bharat Desai	MI	419	13,600
TIBCO Software Inc.	Vivek Ranadive	CA	621.4	2,097
TranSwitch Corporation	Santanu Das	CT	56.1	227
WebEx Communications	Subrah S. Iyar	CA	NA	2,411

Sources: Various public sources, NVCA study, and hoovers.com

Notes: Sales and employment data are the latest available.
Some of these companies have since been acquired by other companies.

Table 5-1 provides a select list of companies founded by Indian immigrants in the United States, along with information on sales and employment. Practically all these companies are in high-tech sectors that pay above-average wages.

Hotel Owners. To anyone who has stayed at hotels/motels in the United States, it may not come as a surprise that Indian Americans are the largest ethnic group of hotel owners in the U.S. According to a recent study by the Atlanta-based PKF Hospitality Research, sponsored by the Asian American Hotel Owners Association (AAHOA), the 10,000 members of AAHOA own 20,156 hotels, which together have 1.8 million rooms and a property value of $129 billion.[xxvi]

Indian Americans own over 40 percent of all hotels in the United States and 39 percent of all guest rooms. They employ 578,600 workers, including the equivalent of 436,900 full-time jobs plus additional part-time employees. Salaries and wages paid to these workers total $9.4 billion annually, plus another $2.5 billion paid in payroll taxes and employee benefits.

Over 95 percent of AAHOA members are Indian Americans. They are "typically small business entrepreneurs, but many have established portfolios that include numerous full-service, limited-service, and independent lodging facilities. They have strong roots in their communities and generate a powerful local 'ripple' economic effect through their expenditure of operating expenses plus capital investments." For instance, AAHOA members spend over $31 billion annually on operating costs such as: wages ($11.9 billion), utilities ($2.3 billion), franchise fees and marketing and reservation expenses ($2.2 billion), property taxes ($2 billion), food and beverage purchases ($1.3 billion), supplies ($1.2 billion), credit card commissions ($1.1 billion), and capital improvements ($900 million).

Indian American Professionals

Indian Americans are contributing to the U.S. economy and society in literally all fields. Here's brief information on, and select lists of, such individuals in different categories.

Physicians. For over 25 years, Indian Americans physicians have been making significant contributions to their communities, to health care, and to the medical profession in the United States – not only practicing in inner cities, rural areas, and peripheral communities, but also at the top medical schools and other academic centers.

The American Association of Physicians of Indian Origin (AAPI) is the largest ethnic medical organization in the United States, second only to the American Medical Association, and represents the interests of more than 50,000 physicians and about 15,000 medical students/residents of Indian heritage in America. Although Indian Americans represent less than one percent of the U.S. population, students of Indian origin constitute 10-12 percent of medical students entering U.S. schools.[xxvii]

The Association (AAPI) currently has 17,441 active members. Table 5-2 on the next page shows the numbers of AAPI members in the Top 15 states, as well as the top 15 specialties of Indian American physicians.

Nobel Laureates. Har Gobind Khurana (Medicine, 1968), Subramanyan Chandrasekhar (Physics, 1983), Amartya Sen (Economics, 1998), and Venkatraman Ramakrishnan (Chemistry, 2009).

Table 5-2: The Number of AAPI Members by State and by Specialty

State	Count
New York	2,365
California	1,534
Illinois	1,456
Ohio	1,258
New Jersey	1,143
Texas	1,105
Michigan	942
Florida	882
Pennsylvania	847
Maryland	560
Indiana	368
Massachusetts	359
Virginia	359
Georgia	348
Missouri	280
Total (U.S.)	**17,441**

Specialty	Count
Internal Medicine	3,204
Pediatrics	1,600
Psychiatry	1,263
Anesthesiology	1,051
Cardiovascular Diseases	996
Obstetrics & Gynecology	597
Pathology	536
Gastroenterology	444
Neurology	373
Family Practice	360
Pulmonary Diseases	328
Diagnostic Radiology	252
Urology	238
Physical Medicine & Rehabilitation	235
Orthopedic Surgery	183
Total (All Specialties)	**17,441**

Source: AAPI

Note: Data shown above do not include the other medical and healthcare professionals of Indian heritage in the United States, such as dentists, pharmacists, and nurses.

CEOs at Major Corporations. Indira Nooyi (PepsiCo), Vikram Pandit (Citigroup), Shantanu Narayen (Adobe Systems), Francisco D'Souza (Cognizant Technology Solutions), Surya Mohapatra (Quest Diaagnostics), Dinesh Paliwal (Harman International), Jai P. Nagarkatti (Sigma-Aldrich), and Abhijit Talwalkar (LSI).[xxviii] There are thousands of other corporate executives of Indian heritage who are senior and top-level executives of medium and large businesses throughout the United States.

Educators. This is also an area where Indian Americans have made major contributions to the United States and to their disciplines. Just to name a few, here's a select list of "college deans" in major business and engineering schools in the United States: G. Anandalingam (Dean, Robert H. Smith School of Business, University of Maryland), Vijay Dhir (Dean, Henry Samueli School of Engineering, UCLA), Pradeep Khosla (Dean of Engineering, Carnegie Mellon University), Nitin Nohria (Dean, Harvard Business School), Shankar Sastry (Dean of Engineering, University of California, Berkeley), and Subra Suresh (Dean of Engineering, Massachusetts Institute of Technology).

Engineers, Scientists, and Technologists. Of the thousands of engineers, scientists, and technologists of Indian heritage in the United States, a special mention must be made of those who graduated from the famed Indian Institutes of Technology (IITs). Most Fortune 500 and other high-technology companies have one or more IITians in their senior executive cadres, so do Wall Street investment banks, federal government agencies like NASA, the World Bank, and so on. There are even management gurus who received their first degree at an IIT. It will be an impossible task to capture the contributions of the IITians to the American economy in a study like this. However, some of their achievements have been documented in publications like *The IITians: The Story of a Remarkable Indian Institution and How Its Alumni Are Reshaping the World* by Sandipan Deb (Penguin/Viking, 2004).

Obama Administration Appointees. A select list of Indian Americans serving in the Obama Administration are: Rajen Anand (Executive Director, Policy, USDA Center for Nutrition and Promotion), Aneesh Chopra (Federal Chief Technology Officer), Ro Khanna (Deputy Assistant Secretary for Domestic Operations, US and Foreign Commercial Service, International Trade Administration), Vivek Kundra (Federal Chief Information Officer), Arun Majumdar (Director, Advanced Research Projects Agency, Department of Energy), Farah Pandith (US Special Representative to Muslim communities), Rajiv Shah (Administrator, U.S. Agency for International Development), Rajiv Shah (Undersecretary for Research, Education & Economics and Chief Scientist, Department of Agriculture), Islam A. Siddiqui (Chief Agricultural Negotiator, Office of the US Trade Representative), Vinai Thummalapally (US envoy to Belize), and Richard Verma (Assistant Secretary for Legislative Affairs, State Department).

Politicians. Bobby Jindal, the Governor of Louisiana, is the highest-profile Indian American in the political sphere in the United States. There are also dozens of state Senators and Assembly men and women as well as city mayors, Council members, and other elected officials of Indian heritage that serve their respective constituencies.

Journalists. They are often the most visible group of Indian Americans in the United States. Some of them are: Falguni Lakhani (Producer, Dateline NBC), Vinita Nair (Anchor, World News Now and America This Morning, ABC), Raju Narisetti (Managing Editor, The Washington Post), Uma Pemmaraju (Senior News Anchor, Fox News Channel), Gopal Raju (Editor, India Abroad, and pioneer of American Indian media in the United States), Shihab Rattansi (CNN International Anchor), Ali Velshi (CNN Business News Anchor), Zain Verjee (CNN Anchor), and Fareed Zakaria (Editor, Newsweek, and host of Fareed Zakaria GPS on CNN).[xxix]

This has necessarily been a very brief listing of Indian Americans and their contributions to the American economy and society. We have had to leave out many prominent Indian Americans and categories, e.g., artists and entertainers, who are also making a difference to America.

Indian Students in the United States

Education is one of America's finest exports and is a trillion dollar industry. The foreign students who come for higher studies to the United States not only bring talent, but also contribute to the U.S. economy via tuition, living and other expenses, and in many other ways. According to the Institute of International Education's just-published *Open Doors 2009* report, the *net (financial) contribution* of foreign students and their families to the U.S. economy in 2008 was over $15.5 billion. Money spent by foreign students and their families in the United States is treated as "deemed exports" from the U.S., which, again, is linked to tens of thousands of American jobs. And, India has had the largest number of foreign students studying in the United States for eight year in a row.[xxx]

There were a total of 671,616 foreign students in the United States in the 2008/09 academic year, of which 103,260 students were from India. In 2008, there were 94,563 students from India who contributed $2.39 billion to the U.S. economy. Table 5-3 shows the net contribution of Indian students in 20 states with large numbers of Indian students in 2008.

Note: Foreign students' net contribution to the U.S. economy includes tuition, living expenses of students and their dependents, *less* support received from U.S. sources. The estimates of net contribution in Table 5-3 were computed based on averages for different states taken from *Open Doors 2008*.

"The vital mortar to seal the bricks of world order is education across international borders, not with the expectation that the knowledge would make us love each other, but in the hope that it would encourage empathy between nations, and foster the emergence of leaders whose sense of other nations and cultures would enable them to share specific policies based on tolerance and rational restraint."

Senator J. William Fulbright

Table 5-3: Net Contribution of Students from India to the Economies of 20 U.S. States with Large Numbers of Indian Students, 2008

State	No. of Students from India	# Indian Students as % of All Foreign Students	Indian Students' Net Contribution ($M)
California	8,299	9.79%	$240
Texas	7,637	14.74%	$156
New York	7,234	10.36%	$202
Illinois	5,906	20.50%	$146
Pennsylvania	4,504	17.26%	$124
Ohio	3,906	20.19%	$87
Massachusetts	3,327	10.46%	$105
Michigan	3,227	14.12%	$74
New Jersey	2,619	19.03%	$76
Indiana	2,592	16.67%	$61
Florida	2,432	9.10%	$61
Connecticut	1,959	24.38%	$60
Virginia	1,935	14.25%	$43
Georgia	1,892	14.32%	$47
North Carolina	1,747	15.94%	$39
Arizona	1,718	17.61%	$35
Missouri	1,697	16.11%	$38
Oklahoma	1,218	14.46%	$24
Maryland	1,133	8.50%	$32
Minnesota	1,040	10.52%	$21
Other States	28,541	21.19%	$722
Total – U.S.	**94,563**	**15.16%**	**$2,393**

Source: Open Doors 2008, Institute of International Education

Appendix: Methodology

This study is based on an extensive amount of research utilizing a variety of data sources, both primary and secondary. The key data sources used were:

Greenfield investment and jobs data were obtained from fDi Intelligence, a service of Financial Times Limited, U.K. which captures such data for most countries. As companies do not always release information on investment amount or job creation, fDi Intelligence uses a proprietary econometric model (patent pending) to estimate the jobs and investments where the actual value is not known. For more information on the methodology used by fDi, please visit: http://www.fdimarkets.com/index.cfm?page_name=markets§ion=faq

M&A data were obtained from several sources, including Thompson's SDC Database, FICCI publications produced jointly with Ernst & Young, publications of Virtus Global Partners, and Prof. Jaya Prakash Pradhan. We merged the FDI information from these sources and verified it through our own research on investment announcements in daily and business press, company Websites, other Internet resources (e.g., Hoovers), and completed survey questionnaires received from some companies. (We had sent out a survey questionnaire to a number of Indian companies operating in the United States, and incorporated the information received from survey respondents in this report). Finally, we did phone or personal interviews with a few companies.

Professor Jaya Prakash Pradhan of the Sardar Patel Institute of Economic & Social Research was kind enough to provide us data on foreign direct investments from India, based on published sources and the Reserve Bank of India (which approves foreign investments by Indian companies). Two of his publications provide more information on his research:

Pradhan, J.P. (2009) 'Indian FDI Falls in Global Economic Crisis: Indian Multinationals Tread Cautiously', *Columbia FDI Perspectives* , No. 11, Columbia Law School and The Earth Institute, Columbia University, August 17. (For M&A Data)

Pradhan, Jaya Prakash (2008): *Indian Direct Investment in Developing Countries: Emerging Trends and Development Impacts.* ISID Working Paper, No. WP2008/08. (For Greenfield Indian FDI Data)

Data on U.S. trade with India and other countries, as well as the numbers of jobs linked to exports, were obtained from two U.S. Department of Commerce Websites:

http://tse.export.gov/
http://www.trade.gov/td/industry/otea/jobs/Reports/2006/jobs_by_state.html

Tables 4-1, 4-2, and 4-3: Exports data were derived from http://tse.export.gov/

The following U.S. Department of Commerce site provides the numbers of jobs linked to exports from the 50 U.S. states and the District of Columbia for Year 2006.

http://www.trade.gov/td/industry/otea/jobs/Reports/2006/jobs_by_state.html

For each state, we computed the ratio of jobs linked to total worldwide merchandise exports from the state in 2006, and then used this ratio for computing jobs linked to exports from that state to India in 2008 (Table 4-4 and 4-5).

Example: California

Total Worldwide Exports (2006):	$127,770,794,000
No. of Jobs Linked to Exports (2006):	691,800
Exports/Jobs:	$184,693.26

Implication: For California, each $184,693 in exports was linked to one job in the state in 2006. (Note: This number is different for different states)

Exports to India (2008):	$2,328,638,000
No. of Jobs Linked to Exports to India (2008):	12,608 (= $2,328,638,000 ÷ $184,693)

Performing the above computation for each state and the District of Columbia, we estimated that a total of 98,292 jobs were linked to total exports ($17,682,085,000) from the United States to India in 2008.

Tables 4-4 and 4-5: We used the ratio (98,292 ÷ $17,682,085,000) to estimate the numbers of jobs for the other years (2004-2007) in Table 4-4 and 4-5. These estimates include jobs in both manufacturing and non-manufacturing occupations linked to manufactured exports to India, and do not include jobs linked to non-manufactured exports, such as agricultural and mineral products, and services exports.

Disclaimer: This report was developed based largely on secondary sources of information (plus some primary sources, including information provided by some of the companies included in the report). While care has been taken to be as accurate as possible in reporting this information, the authors, the India-US World Affairs Institute, FICCI, and the Robert H. Smith School of Business, University of Maryland accept no responsibility for the accuracy or otherwise of the contents of this report. The opinions expressed in this report are those of the authors and not of any of the study's sponsors.

Acknowledgements

A project like this could not have been completed without the active support and cooperation of a lot of individuals and organizations. In view of space limitation, we can acknowledge only some of them. However, we offer our gratitude to everyone who contributed to the study, whether or not they are identified here.

The project got a head start when the authors met with Ranjana Khanna, FICCI's Deputy Secretary General based in Washington D.C., who provided a broad outline of what the study could cover and also provided us with contact information for dozens of Indian companies in the United States. We also received encouragement for the study when we met with FICCI Secretary General, Dr. Amit Mitra, V.K. Topa, Advisor to the Secretary General, Ashok Ummat, Executive Director, and Sunita Rattan, Senior Assistant Director for Americas at FICCI headquarters in New Delhi in August 2009. Our grateful thanks to all of them.

A number of other individuals and organizations provided a good deal of information for the study, for which we are thankful to them. These include Professor Jaya Prakash Pradhan of the Sardar Patel Institute of Economic & Social Research; Dr. Vinod Shah, the current president of the American Association of Physicians of Indian Origin (AAPI), and Ms. Vijaya Kodali, also of AAPI; Mr. Fred Schwartz, President, and Mr. Chris Carlson, P.R. and Communications Manager, of the Asian American Hotel Owners Association; and Mr. Gunjan Bagla, President of PanIIT, the worldwide association of IIT alumni. Mahdi Zanddizari, Vinod's Graduate Assistant at the Smith School, did a good amount of work to develop lists of Indian companies investing in the United States based on library databases and Google searches.

Many other individuals and companies provided information about their U.S. operations in our survey of Indian companies in the United States, which provided depth to our analysis and a check on the data we collected from secondary sources. These are: Hiranya Ashar (Rolta); Raghu Balakrishnan (Polaris Software); Chuck Caprariello (Ranbaxy); Avisek Das, David Good, and Anjali Sharan (Tata); Rajesh Nair (Indegene/ILSL Holdings); Murali Ramanathan (Jain Americas); Rajesh Sinha (Thermax); Greg Tilley (Infotech Enterprises); and Josh Wendroff (3i Infotech); among others. Thank you.

Finally, we received an incredible amount of help from our daughters, Sumita and Anupama, who spent days with us, in person and virtually, researching, editing, and contributing to the study in numerous ways. Sumita and Anu, this could not have been done without you! Thank you!

Vinod K. Jain
Kamlesh Jain

About the Authors

Vinod Jain is professor and associate director of research at the Robert H. Smith School of Business, University of Maryland, and President and CEO of India-US World Affairs Institute, Inc. A true cosmopolitan and Fulbright Scholar, Vinod has lived and worked in India, the United States, Western Europe, Eastern Europe, China, and the Middle East. During the last ten years, he has received and managed five competitive grants from the U.S. Department of Education, including a $1.43 million grant in 2006 to establish the Center for International Business Education & Research at the University of Maryland, which he headed until February 2009.

Vinod teaches "*strategy*", "*global strategy*", and "*emerging markets*" on Smith School's MBA program, and "*strategy*" at the University of Lodz in Poland. He has also taught on Smith School's Executive MBA program in China and Switzerland. His current research involves measuring regional innovation in the United States, a project funded partially by the IBM Center for the Business of Government. Prior to returning to academia in 1990, Vinod worked in industry for some fifteen years and held a variety of middle and senior executive positions with multinational corporations. And, he has been honored by the Governors of both Ohio (2001) and Maryland (2004) for his services to their states. He has a Ph.D. in business and management from the University of Maryland and Master's degrees in Management (UCLA) and Statistics (Indian Statistical Institute). He serves on the Maryland/Washington D.C. District Export Council, to which he was appointed by the Secretary, U.S. Department of Commerce in 2008. He is a member of the Academy of International Business, Academy of Management, Mensa, and the Asia Society.

Kamlesh Jain is Director of Research & Education at the India-US World Affairs Institute. Prior to her current position, she worked for the U.S. Department of the Treasury for six years, first in the Office of Research and then in Corporate Performance Budgeting, in positions such as Section Chief for the Operating Divisions Office and Supervisory Budget Analyst. She has also taught at several universities in the United States and abroad, including University of Maryland, College Park, University of Texas at Dallas, and the University of Aston in Birmingham, U.K. She headed the training function at the Industrial Finance Corporation of India, Mumbai, and Tata Consultancy Services, New Delhi, while based in India in the 1980s. She has a Ph.D. in Management Science/Statistics from University of Maryland, a Master's in Management from UCLA, and an Honors Bachelor's and a Master's degrees in Statistics from the Indian Statistical Institute.

India-US World Affairs Institute, Inc.

Founded in 2006, the India-US World Affairs Institute, Inc. is an independent, non-profit, tax-exempt 501(c)(3) institution dedicated to promoting understanding and positive relationships between and among the peoples of India, the United States, and the world – through education, experiential learning, research, thought leadership, publications, seminars, conferences, travel and study abroad, and strategic partnerships.

Our mission is to encourage individuals and organizations transcend boundaries – physical, social, and cultural – to improve their global bandwidth. Our members, staff, board of advisors, board of directors, and alumni constitute a global network of men and women with diverse professional backgrounds and global expertise in areas such as society, culture, foreign affairs, economics, economic development, global business, and strategy and competitiveness. For more information, please visit www.india-us.org or contact: vjain@india-us.org.

Federation of Indian Chambers of Commerce & Industry

Established in 1927, FICCI is the largest and oldest apex business organization in India. Its history is closely interwoven with India's struggle for independence and its subsequent emergence as one of the most rapidly growing economies globally. FICCI plays a leading role in policy debates that are at the forefront of social, economic and political change. Through its FICCI is active in 39 sectors of the Indian economy and its stand on policy issues is sought out by think tanks, governments, and academia.

FICCI has direct membership from the private as well as public sectors, including SMEs and MNCs, and an indirect membership of over 83,000 companies from regional chambers of commerce. FICCI is headquartered in New Delhi and has eight regional offices throughout India and six overseas offices, including one in Washington, D.C.

Robert H. Smith School of Business, University of Maryland

The Robert H. Smith School of Business at University of Maryland is an internationally recognized leader in management education and research. A comprehensive business school, Smith offers undergraduate, full-time and part-time MBA, Executive MBA, PhD, and non-degree executive education programs, as well research and outreach services to the corporate community. Smith School is one of only a few schools of business in the world to be ranked in the top schools for both research and teaching.

Smith School is one of 13 schools and colleges that comprise the University of Maryland, College Park, the only highly ranked, comprehensive, and research-focused university in the National Capital Area.

What can we do for you?

The India-US World Affairs Institute Inc. is the only Washington D.C.-based independent, non-profit educational and research institution dedicated to promoting understanding and positive relationships between and amongst the peoples of India, the United States, and the world. Our members, staff, board of directors, board of advisors, and alumni constitute a global network of men and women with diverse professional backgrounds and global expertise in areas such as society, culture, education, foreign affairs, economics, economic development, global business, technology, innovation, and strategy and competitiveness.

Educational Institutions

With the coming changes in legislation, India offers opportunities for foreign universities interested in establishing a beachhead in India. We offer the following services for American universities.

- Find strategic partners in India – for joint educational and research programs, student and faculty exchanges, company visits, and corporate internships
- Design and lead study abroad programs in India for students/faculty, including programs with built-in internships or project work for students, as well as immersion experiences in India

We also offer similar services for Indian universities interested in the United States.

Economic Development Organizations

We assist economic development organizations from the United States seek out Indian companies interested in investing in their jurisdictions, and U.S. companies seeking to build strategic alliance or joint venture with Indian companies.

We also offer similar services for economic development organizations and corporations in India interested in exploring the U.S. marketplace.

Corporations

A small sampling of educational seminars our staff and board members have offered in the past:

- Doing Business in India
- Doing Business in America
- The Bangalore Seminar
- The Washington Seminar
- Executive Leadership
- Global Strategy
- Competing and Winning in Emerging Market

For more information, please visit www.india-us.org, or contact President@india-us.org

Endnotes

[i] David Griswold, *Mad About Trade: Why Mainstreet America Should Embrace Globalization*, Cato Institute, 2009.

[ii] http://minnesota.publicradio.org/display/web/2008/09/19/steelplantopens/

[iii] Based on: David Griswold, 2009.

[iv] Authors' interview with company management.

[v] http://abcnews.go.com/Politics/obama-travels-asia-climate-change-north-korea-trade/story?id=9053006

[vi] http://www.opendoors.iienetwork.org

[vii] N.S.B. Gras, "A Great Indian Industrialist: Jamsetji Nusserwanji Tata, 1839-1904", *Bulletin of the Business Historical Society*, 23(3), 1949.

[viii] Ann Graham, "Too Good to Fail", *Strategy+Business*, Spring 2010.

[ix] Source: http://northamerica.tata.com

[x] Ravi Ramamurti and Jitendra V. Singh, "Indian Multinationals: Generic Internationalization Strategies." In Ravi Ramamurti & Jitendra V. Singh (eds.), *Emerging Multinationals from Emerging Markets*, Ch. 6, Cambridge University Press, 2008.

[xi] For business and financial market sophistication, India ranks very high among all countries, not just among developing countries, in the Global Competitiveness Index, 2009-2010 (World Economic Forum).

[xii] IMaCS VIRTUS Global Partners, US-Bound Acquisitions by Indian Companies, January 2010.

[xiii] http://www.unctad.org/Templates/WebFlyer.asp?intItemID=3968&lang=1

[xiv] www.fdiintelligence.com

[xv] http://www.unctad.org/wir

[xvi] http://www.tradeandindustrydev.com/ID-897-news.aspx

[xvii] Antoine van Agtmael, *The Emerging Markets Century: How a New Breed of World-Class Companies is Overtaking the World*, Free Press, 2007

[xviii] Amit Mitra, "N-Power to Brain Power", *Hindustan Times*, October 23, 2009, http://www.hindustantimes.com/StoryPage/Print/468167.aspxx

[xix] Employment Related to Manufactured Exports, 2006, U.S. Department of Commerce, International Trade Administration: http://www.trade.gov/td/industry/otea/jobs/Reports/2006/jobs_by_state.html. These data do not include jobs involved in the export of non-manufactured goods, such as farm

products, minerals, and services sold to foreign buyers. The results are based on the 2006 Annual Survey of Manufactures, conducted by the Bureau of the Census, U.S. Department of Commerce.

[xx] The sonnet is inscribed on a bronze plaque in an exhibit on the second floor of the pedestal to the Statue of Liberty in New York Harbor.

[xxi] The term, "brain drain" was coined to refer to such emigration from developing countries such as India. In recent years, however, there have been tens of thousands cases of "reverse brain drain" when people from India and China returned to their home countries as economic conditions improved there.

[xxii] The Census Bureau uses the "Asian Indian" terminology to refer to people from Indian origin in the United States.

[xxiii] The 2005 American Community Survey: http://factfinder.census.gov/servlet/IPTable?_bm=y&-geo_id=01000US&-qr_name=ACS_2005_EST_G00_S0201&-qr_name=ACS_2005_EST_G00_S0201PR&-qr_name=ACS_2005_EST_G00_S0201T&-qr_name=ACS_2005_EST_G00_S0201TPR&-reg=ACS_2005_EST_G00_S0201:032;ACS_2005_EST_G00_S0201PR:032;ACS_2005_EST_G00_S0201T:032;ACS_2005_EST_G00_S0201TPR:032&-ds_name=ACS_2005_EST_G00_&-_lang=en&-format=

[xxiv] Wadhwa et al. (2007). America's New Immigrant Entrepreneurs: Part I. http://papers.ssrn.com/sol3/papers.cfm?abstract_id=990152

[xxv] http://www.nfap.com/researchactivities/studies/immigrant_entreprenuers_professionals_november_2006.pdf

[xxvi] http://www.aahoa.com/AM/Template.cfm?Section=Press_Releases1&TEMPLATE=/CM/ContentDisplay.cfm&CONTENTID=4717

[xxvii] http://www.aapiusa.org/

[xxviii] http://www.forbes.com/2009/12/17/indian-ceos-united-states-forbes-asia-indian-ceos.html

[xxix] http://en.wikipedia.org/wiki/List_of_Indian_Americans#Academic

[xxx] http://www.opendoors.iienetwork.org

www.ingramcontent.com/pod-product-compliance
Lightning Source LLC
LaVergne TN
LVHW070143110826
845147LV00002B/314